KU-301-074

WITHDRAWN

1/1

Birkhäuser – Publishers for Architecture
Basel · Boston · Berlin

Ingenhoven Overdiek und Partner / KMS Team
Architektur und Design: Neue Synergien / Architecture and Design: New Synergies
Mit einem Essay von Robert Wilson / With an Essay by Robert Wilson

1/1

WITHDRAWN

m 721 ING

7dy

WITHDRAWN

Robert Wilson / I remember …

WITHDRAWN

I remember Reading Edwin Denby's
dance criticisms in the early 60's.
In his writings he asked questions,
in other words he would ask: s
        WHAT IS IT
            AND NOT
        WHAT IT IS
this was a confirmation for me to
work as an artist.

I remember FirSt Seeing George Balanchine
ballets, I was attracted to the M
                                    E
                                    N
LANdscape he created, and the FREEdoM T
                                        A
                                        L
I experienced in having the work formally
presented in Abstract classical patterns
his stage space Allowed the public to go
to the PerfOrmer because the perfOrmer
was not demanding the Public's attention.

I rEMEmbeR theBst CLASS I EveR HAd
iN SCHOOL wAS tAught bY SyBiL
MOHOLY-NAGY. It HAPPeNEd iN the 3rd
YEAR oFA 5 YEAR COURSe iN the HISTORY oF
ARCHiteCtURe. WE WERE ASKEd tO deSiGN
A CiTY iN 3 MiNUTeS, AND I dREw AN APPLE
WitH A CRYStAL CUbE iN Side. I WAS
thiNKiNG tHAt   OUR COMMUNITieS
Need CENTeRS,   LiKE tHE CRYStAL
CUbE At the   CORE OF AN
APPLE REFLECTiNG tHE UNiVERSe, LiKEA
MEDiEVAL CiTY witH A CAtHedRAL iN tHE
CENTER OF tHe ViLLAGE, A PLACE wHeRe
PEOPLE COUld CONGREGATE FOR LEARNiNG,
UNdERStANDiNG AND EN LiGHTenment.

I rEMEmbeR iN THE 70's PERFORMING witH
CHRIStOPHeR KNOwLeS iN SHiRAZ, At tHe
eNd OF tHe PERFORMANCE, CHRiS SPontANesLy
SPoKe + tHe WORD "TAPe-RECORDeR" TAPE reretAPr
+ tA + TAPE TAPe-Recorder +TAPE RECORd ddd r
  + e tAE   e ++   d
         e   +

FOR 10 MINUTES. AS WE WERE LEAVING
the STAGE the AuDIENCe ONLY CAUGHED.
tHERE WAS NO APPLAUSe, AND CHRIS SAID:

"who cares to have your mind be so smooth"

I rEMEMbeR MARCeL BREUER SAYING
tHAT iN tHe CHAIRS He deSIGNed WERE ALL
HiS AEStHETiCS. tHE SAMEAEStHEtiCS
tHAT GO iNto DESIGNING A builDING. tHe
SAME AEStHetiCS tHAT go iNto dESIGNiNG A
CITY.

I rEMEMbeR BARNEtt NEWMAN SAYING
to HiS wife AnnALee WHEN SHOWING HER
FOR tHE 1st TiME A LARGe HORiZONtAL
CANVAS PAINted RED
" LOOK HOW FAR I StRetCHed it "

I rEMEMbeR iN tHe 80'S WHEN JESSYE NORMAN
WAS ASKED ON A TALK SHOW WHAt HER FAVORite
reCOrdING WAS AND SHE rePLied:
" I HAVE A DREAM "

Martin Luther King

I rEmEmbeR the text david byRNE wRote FoR ouR collAboRAtion FoR the "KNEE PLAYS" iN "the CIVIL WARS, A tree is best meAsured WHEN IT is down "

IN THE FUTURE   everyone wiLL HAVE THE SAME HAIRCUT AND THE SAME CLOTHES

IN THE FUTURE   IT WILL BE IMPOSSIBLE TO TELL GIRLS FROM BOYS

IN THE FUTURE   MEN WILL BE "SUPER-MASCULINE" AND WOMEN WILL BE "ULTRA-FEMININE"

IN THE FUTURE   THE WEATHER WILL ALWAYS BE THE SAME. (RELATIVE TO THE WAY IT IS NOW)

IN THE FUTURE   WATER WILL BE EXPENSIVE

IN THE FUTURE   ALL MATERIAL ITEMS WILL BE FREE.

IN THE FUTURE   EVERYONE WILL STAY HOME ALL THE TIME

IN THE FUTURE   THERE WILL ONLY BE PAPER MONEY, WHICH WILL BE PERSONALIZED

IN THE FUTURE THERE WILL BE SO MUCH GOING ON THAT NO ONE WILL BE ABLE TO KEEP TRACK OF IT

IN THE FUTURE EVERYONE WILL BE VERY FAT FROM THE STARCHY DIET

IN THE FUTURE EVERYONE WILL BE VERY THIN FROM NOT HAVING ENOUGH TO EAT T T

Robert Wilson
WATERMILL CENTER
August 5, 2000

Der Auftritt von Audi auf der Internationalen Automobil-Ausstellung 1999 in Frankfurt hat in der Fachwelt Aufsehen erregt. Nicht nur wegen des betriebenen Aufwands, sondern auch wegen der neuen Art der Kooperation zwischen Architekten und Kommunikationsdesignern. Mussten Sie dafür den Umgang miteinander erst lernen?

Ingenhoven / Wenn unterschiedliche Denkmuster und Berufstraditionen aufeinander treffen, gibt es natürlich ein paar Verständigungsschwierigkeiten. Mir ist erst gegen Ende unserer Zusammenarbeit klar geworden, dass Architekten ganz andere Lösungsstrategien verfolgen – schon allein deswegen, weil sie sich mit voluminöseren Objekten beschäftigen. Sie entwickeln nicht nur einen entwerferischen und künstlerischen Ansatz, sondern unterlegen dem Planungsprozess auch eine organisatorische Strategie, die eine große Einheit in kleine Teile zerlegt. Und neigen möglicherweise zur Arroganz, das Design für eines dieser kleinen Teile zu halten …

Keller / … während wir uns ja ebenfalls als Regisseure verstehen. Das ist unter anderem ein Wahrnehmungsproblem, das sicher mit dem diffusen Berufsbild zu tun hat, das wir in der Öffentlichkeit haben. Unter der Arbeit eines Architekten kann sich jeder etwas vorstellen. Aber was ist, wenn ich sage, ich sei Kommunikationsdesigner? Bin ich der Mann, der die Visitenkarten macht? Die Werbung? Das Licht? Oder die Clips, die man im Fernsehen sieht? Das sind verbreitete Missverständnisse, und es ist kein Zufall, dass Christoph Ingenhoven anfangs immer von KMS als von einer Werbeagentur gesprochen hat. In Wirklichkeit hat unsere Arbeit sehr viele Parallelen zu der des Architekten, auch wenn diese nicht so offensichtlich sein mögen. Die Entwicklung und Umsetzung eines schlüssigen Kommunikationskonzepts verlangt nicht nur Kreativität, sondern auch ein hohes Maß an Planung, Organisation und Führung.

Audi's entry at the Frankfurt International Auto Show in 1999 caused quite a sensation among the experts. This was not only due to the lavish expenditure but also because of a new type of cooperation between architects and communications designers. Did this involve a learning experience in the interactions with your colleagues?

Ingenhoven / Whenever different ways of thinking and professional traditions come together, there are naturally going to be a few problems of communication. I only realized toward the end of our cooperation that architects pursue a very different set of strategies in their solutions—not least because they deal with more voluminous objects. Architects not only develop an approach in terms of artistic design, they also base the planning process on an organizational strategy of breaking large units down into small components. And they possibly tend toward the arrogant view that design is but one of these small components …

Keller / … while we, of course, likewise think of ourselves as directors. This is partly a problem of perception, one that is certainly connected with the vague professional image we have in the eyes of the public. Everyone has some idea of the work of an architect. But what if I say that I'm a communications designer? Am I the guy who makes the business cards? The ads? The lighting design? Or the clips you see on television? These are common misconceptions, and it is not by accident that Christoph Ingenhoven initially always spoke of KMS as an advertising agency. In reality, our work has many parallels to the work of architects, even though these may not be very obvious. The development and realization of a coherent communications concept not only requires creativity but also a high degree of planning, organization and leadership.

Ingenhoven / Wenn man sich die Geschichte des Berufes anschaut, war der Architekt schon immer ein Generalist. Ursprünglich übte er eine Art handwerklicher Tätigkeit aus, aber bereits im Laufe des Mittelalters war er, wenn man an die Dombauten denkt, ein Koordinator der Steinmetz- und der anderen Bauarbeiten. Er musste ein großes Wissen in sich vereinigen, konnte sich aber auf die spezifischen handwerklichen und technischen Fähigkeiten vieler anderer verlassen, die jeweils ihre eigene Berufstradition hatten. Auch im 19. Jahrhundert, zu Zeiten Schinkels, gab es noch den Anspruch des Architekten, Universaldesigner zu sein. Er arbeitete in einem Team, in welchem er der einzige Planer war, ansonsten aber nicht streng zwischen Planen und Bauen unterschieden wurde. Mit der Industrialisierung setzte eine starke Spezialisierung der Berufe ein. Damit änderte sich auch der des Architekten.

Dieser ursprüngliche Aufgabenbereich hat sich ja mittlerweile stark aufgefächert …

Ingenhoven / Heute arbeitet eine Vielzahl von Spezialisten in der Planerriege am Bau: Tragwerksplaner, Bauphysiker, Fassadenkonstrukteure, Haustechniker, Klimaingenieure. Früher gab es einen Architekten, heute mehr als ein Dutzend Disziplinen. Das macht den Planungsprozess divergent und vergrößert auch die Distanz zwischen Planern und Handwerkern. Ich mag es, im Team zu entwerfen und zu erfinden.

Ingenhoven / If you look at the history of the profession, architects were always generalists. Originally, the architect practiced a type of skilled trade. Already in the course of the Middle Ages, however, architects coordinated the work of stonemasons and other building trades in the construction of cathedrals, for example. An architect had to integrate a great amount of knowledge but was able to rely on the specific technical and craft skills of numerous other people, with their own particular professional traditions. Still in the 19th century, at the time of Schinkel, architects claimed to be universal designers. The architect worked in a team, in which he was the only planner, and in which otherwise there was no strict distinction between planning and building. Industrialization brought a high degree of professional specialization in its wake. This also transformed the profession of the architect.

In the meantime, this original area of responsibility has developed into many separate domains …

Ingenhoven / In today's construction projects, a great number of specialists work in the planning squad: supporting framework planners, construction physicists, façade builders, building engineers, air conditioning engineers. Where there used to be one architect, there are now more than a dozen disciplines. This results in a divergent planning process and a greater distance between planners and trades people. I enjoy designing and inventing in a team.

Keller / Where, however, in accordance with your self-image, you continue to take on the leading role and do not tolerate any other gods beside yourself …

Keller / Wobei Sie aber nach Ihrem Selbstverständnis weiterhin die führende Rolle übernehmen und keine Götter neben sich dulden …

Ingenhoven / Architektur ist immer eine Art Ego-Drama, und nicht zuletzt sind Architekten oft egomanische Charaktere, denken Sie etwa an Frank Lloyd Wright. Und jetzt kommen plötzlich andere Professionen hinzu, von Fall zu Fall beispielsweise Philosophen, Museumsexperten oder eben Kommunikationsdesigner. Möglicherweise wird ihre Rolle so wichtig werden, dass sie nicht mehr einer unter vielen sind, sondern die eine Position neben der des Architekten innehaben. Das zu akzeptieren fällt Architekten schwer, weil sie Gleichberechtigung nicht gewohnt sind.

Auch der Ursprung Ihres Berufes war, wenn man so will, das Handwerk.

Keller / Ich mag die Betonung des Handwerklichen. Wir kommen von der Buchkunst, zumindest haben wir das anfänglich gelernt: mit Papier umzugehen, mit Schriften, mit Farben und Bildern. Schließlich nannte man unser Fach früher »Graphik-Design«. Doch heute heißt das Thema: Wie inszeniert man etwas? Wie macht man eine Idee, einen bestimmten Geist erlebbar? Otl Aicher hat sich das gefragt, als es um die Olympischen Spiele ging, und hat seine Arbeit gleichsam aus dem Zweidimensionalen herausgehoben. Das war die Initialzündung, Ende der 60er Jahre. Danach hat sich unser Fach rasant entwickelt. Die eher statische Linie der Typographie und Illustration ist mit völlig anderen Traditionen zusammengekommen wie dem Theater, den höfischen Festen, den Fastnachts- und Osterspielen – und andererseits mit dem noch sehr jungen Multimedia-Bereich.

Ingenhoven / Architecture is always a kind of ego-drama. Architects, after all, are often egomaniacs—just take Frank Lloyd Wright as an example. And now, suddenly, other professions enter the scene. Depending on the type of project, these could be philosophers, museum experts or, as in our case, communications designers. Their role could eventually become so important that they are no longer just one among many, but rather occupy the position beside that of the architect. For architects, this is difficult to accept, since they are not used to the idea of equal rights.

The origin of your profession was also a skilled trade, if you will.

Keller / I like the emphasis on handicraft skills. We come from the art of book-making. Or at least this is what we learnt initially: how to handle paper, fonts, colors and images. Our trade, after all, used to be called 'graphic design'. Today, however, the dominant theme is: how do you stage something? How do you generate the experience of an idea or of a certain spirit? Otl Aicher asked himself this question in dealing with the Olympic Games. And he lifted his work out of the two-dimensional plane, as it were. This sparked it all off at the end of the 60s. After that our field developed with lightning speed. The rather static line of typography and illustration merged with completely different traditions such as theater, courtly festivals, carnival and Easter plays—and, on the other hand, with the fledgling field of multimedia.

Kommt jetzt eine neue Welle von Designern, die einen Universalitätsanspruch vertreten?

Keller / Unsere Arbeit hat sich extrem verlagert. Durch die neuen Kommunikationstechniken sind völlig andere Möglichkeiten entstanden – und die Erwartungshaltung hat sich entsprechend verändert. Heute will zum Beispiel der Restaurantbesitzer nicht mehr von uns, dass wir die Visitenkarten machen, den Schriftzug entwickeln oder einen Namen finden. Heute sagt er: »Mach das Restaurant.«

Ingenhoven / Aber das Bauen übernehmt ihr noch nicht …

Keller / Noch nicht (*lacht*) … dafür engagieren wir fähige Architekten. – Aber apropos neue Generation: Hier sehe ich zwischen Europa und Amerika wegen der unterschiedlichen Fachdidaktik eine große Kluft entstehen. Die Design-Studenten setzen dort ihren Studienplan selber zusammen und belegen Kurse in Kunst, Kommunikation, Musik, Philosophie, Medien, BWL. Mit 24 verlassen sie die Uni mit einem weitem Horizont und einiger Selbstsicherheit. Hier dagegen lernen sie weiterhin, Aquarell zu malen und Typographie zu kleben, und sind erst mit 28 fertig … So entsteht beim rasanten Wandel unserer Branche ein immer größerer Abstand zwischen ihren Fähigkeiten und den eigentlichen Aufgaben, die sie erwarten.

Should we expect a new wave of designers that lays claim to universality?

Keller / Our work has shifted dramatically. New communications technologies have created completely different possibilities—and expectations have changed accordingly. Today, for example, a restaurant owner no longer wants us to create the business cards, to develop the logo or to find a name. Today, he simply says: "Create the restaurant".

Ingenhoven / But you do not yet take care of the construction…

Keller / Not yet (*laughing*) … we hire capable architects for this purpose— But speaking of a new generation: I see a large gap arising between Europe and America because of the diverging teaching methods. In America, design students put together their own course of studies, taking classes in fine art, communication, music, philosophy, media, business administration. At age 24, they leave the university with a broad horizon and a certain degree of self-confidence. Here, by contrast, students continue to learn how to draw in water-color and to paste typography and only complete their studies at the age of 28 … And, with the rapid transformation of our field, this results in an ever widening gulf between their skills and the actual tasks that await them.

Welche Aufgaben sind das?

Keller / Wir kümmern uns um Dinge, die – um beim Restaurantbeispiel zu bleiben – wesentlich über die Gestaltung der Speisekarte hinausgehen. Die Fragen
lauten: Wie fühle ich mich, wenn ich im Restaurant bin? Wie sitze ich am Tisch?
Wie werde ich angesprochen? Darf ich in die Küche schauen? Gibt es Musik,
und wenn ja, welche? Wie ist das Gedeck? Wie sind die Toiletten? Das gehört
alles zur Kommunikation.

Gilt das auch für den Messeauftritt von Audi?

Keller / Selbstverständlich. Nur um die Toiletten haben wir uns da nicht geküm-
mert, die werden zentral von der Messegesellschaft betrieben.

Wie war die Aufgabenteilung bei Ihrer Zusammenarbeit?

Keller / Ich würde es auf eine einfache Formel bringen: KMS hat die Software
gemacht, das Büro Ingenhoven die Hardware.

Ingenhoven / Mit dieser Zuordnung bin ich nicht ganz einverstanden. Darin liegt
wohl ein Teil des Konfliktpotentials zwischen Kommunikationsdesignern und
Architekten: die Konkurrenz um den Universalitätsanspruch. Regisseure haben
nun einmal einen Hang zur Dominanz. Ob gut oder mittelmäßig, ob freundlich
oder arrogant, ob gebildet oder nicht – dominant müssen sie stets sein.

What are these tasks?

Keller / We are responsible for things that—if we stay with the example of the restaurant—go much beyond the layout of the menu. The questions are: how do I feel, when I'm in the restaurant? How am I sitting at the table? How am I being addressed? Am I allowed to look into the kitchen? Is there music, and if so, what kind? How are the place settings? How are the restrooms? All of this is part of communication.

Is this also true of Audi's exhibit at the Auto Show?

Keller / Of course, it is. Only the restrooms were not our responsibility, since they are centrally operated by the trade fair corporation.

How were the tasks distributed in your cooperative effort?

Keller / I would bring it down to the simple formula: KMS produced the software, while the Ingenhoven firm produced the hardware.

Ingenhoven / I do not quite agree with this assignment. And herein seems to lie part of the potential for conflict between communications designers and architects: the competition over the claim to universality. Directors, after all, have a tendency to dominate. Whether they are good or mediocre, friendly or arrogant, educated or not—they always have to be dominant.

Gilt das auch für Sie?

Keller / (*lacht*) Für wen?

Ingenhoven / Vermutlich für beide. Aber ich wollte auf etwas Generelles hinaus. Die klassische Haltung des Architekten würde lauten: »Otl Aicher mag ja ein berühmter Mann sein, aber das Olympiastadion hat Günter Behnisch gebaut.« Und egal, wer das Verdienst für sich beanspruchen kann, die Olympischen Spiele gemacht zu haben – das heute noch sichtbare Zeugnis hat tatsächlich Behnisch geschaffen.

Keller / Also doch die Hardware …

Ingenhoven / Wie gesagt, das ist die Sicht der Dinge, die man als Architekt antrainiert bekommt und die ich zunächst auch als selbstverständlich übernommen habe. Inzwischen glaube ich, dass es Formen gleichberechtigter Kooperation und gegenseitiger Befruchtung geben kann, bei denen man zusammen etwas Besseres zustande bringt als jeder Einzelne für sich.

Keller / Ich würde Otl Aichers Einfluss auch nicht höher bewerten als den von Günter Behnisch oder Frei Otto. Ihre Zusammenarbeit ist ein gutes Beispiel für unser Thema. Der Erfolg war das Ergebnis der Synergie, die sie freigesetzt haben.

Does this apply to you as well?

Keller (*laughing*) / To whom?

Ingenhoven / Presumably to both. But I was aiming at a general point. The classical attitude of an architect would be: "Otl Aicher may be a famous man, but the Olympic Stadium was built by Günter Behnisch." And regardless of who may personally take credit for having staged the Olympic Games—the evidence that is still visible today was indeed created by Behnisch.

Keller / Thus, it is the hardware after all …

Ingenhoven / As I said, this is the view one is trained to take as an architect, and one that I initially also assumed as a matter of course. Now I believe that forms of cooperation as equals and of mutual inspiration are possible, where together you produce something better than you would, if each person worked in isolation.

Keller / I would also not rate Otl Aicher's influence higher than that of Günter Behnisch or Frei Otto. Their cooperation is a good example of our topic. Their success was the result of the synergy, which they released.

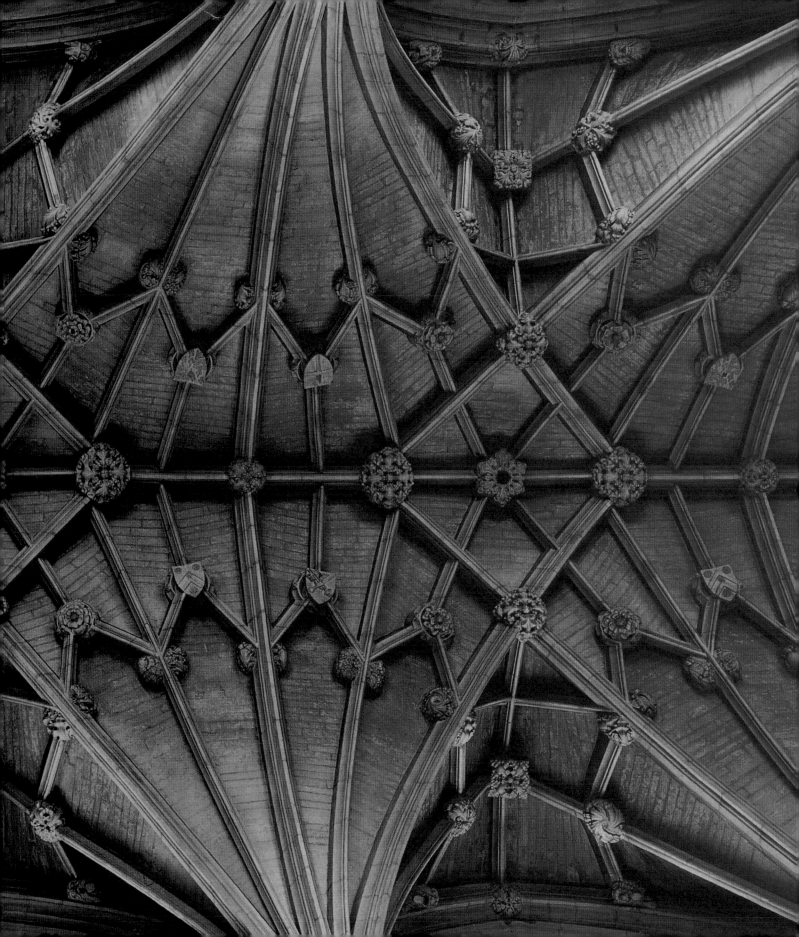

Wie ist Ihre Kooperation für Audi zustandegekommen? War die Gleichberechtigung von vornherein auch formal verankert?

Ingenhoven / Ja und nein, wir haben die jeweilige Zuständigkeit erst einmal ausloten müssen. Aber auf jeden Fall war KMS zuerst da.

Keller / Wir hatten von Audi den Auftrag bekommen, den weltweiten Messeauftritten ein klares Erscheinungsbild zu geben, eine Einheit von Architektur und Kommunikation herzustellen. Und da man uns offensichtlich am meisten zutraute, die Ziele zu formulieren, haben wir insgesamt 27 Architekten in ganz Europa besucht und fünf davon zu einem Wettbewerb eingeladen.

Ingenhoven / Das allein ist übrigens schon sehr bemerkenswert. Architekten sind es gewohnt, dass der Bauherr an sie herantritt, nicht aber, dass jemand Drittes als unabhängige Instanz auch noch dabei ist.

Keller / Dementsprechend war die Aufnahme oft – na ja, nicht unbedingt unfreundlich, aber mit einem großen Fragezeichen versehen: »Wer seid ihr denn?« Das ist keine Arroganz, sondern eher das Symptom eines generellen Problems: Die meisten renommierten Architekten haben bereits eine klare Vorstellung davon, wie das Bauwerk aussehen soll, wenn der Auftraggeber zur Tür hereinkommt. Sie haben ein Markenzeichen und prägen es jedem neuen Entwurf auf. Wozu dann noch andere Gestalter? Christoph Ingenhoven war eine Ausnahme.

Ingenhoven / Das sagen Sie jetzt so.

How did your cooperation for Audi come about? And was the idea of equality also formally embodied from the start?

Ingenhoven / Yes and no. We first had to sound out the respective responsibilities. In any case, KMS was first on the scene.

Keller / We had been commissioned by Audi to give their worldwide auto show exhibits a distinct look, to create a unity of architecture and communication. And since we were evidently most trusted to formulate the goals, we visited a total of 27 architects all over Europe and invited five of them to a competition.

Ingenhoven / This alone is already very remarkable. Architects are used to being approached by the client, but they are not used to the presence of a third party as an independent agent.

Keller / Accordingly, the reception was often—well, not necessarily unfriendly, but accompanied by a big question mark: "And who are you?" This is not arrogance, but rather the symptom of a general problem: most renowned architects already have a clear idea of how the building should look, when the client enters the door. They have a trade mark and leave it on every new design. Why then would you still need other designers? Christoph Ingenhoven was an exception.

Ingenhoven / You say that now.

Keller / Ich meine das auch so. Zumindest was die Bereitschaft angeht, sich auf ein Experiment einzulassen. Die war von Anfang an zu spüren. Und noch eins, falls Sie so viel Lob aus meinem Mund vertragen: Im Gegensatz zu den meisten Ihrer Kollegen hatten Sie Recherchen angestellt und wussten über die aktuellen Produkte bei Audi Bescheid.

War dies das ausschlaggebende Kriterium?

Keller / Nein, aber es war ein gutes Vorzeichen. Allerdings wussten wir ja noch nicht, wie die architektonische Lösung aussehen würde. Und auch als er gegen vier andere Büros zur Endausscheidung in Ingolstadt antrat, war noch nicht klar, was herauskommen würde, wenn wir zusammen arbeiteten.

Ingenhoven / Wegen der Art des Auswahlverfahrens war es auch nicht möglich, die Kooperation zu testen.

Keller / Was recht mutig war. Wir haben uns während der zwei Monate vor der Präsentation völlig unparteiisch verhalten – oder genauer: zurückgehalten. Das war keine leichte Übung.

Ingenhoven / Das Kommunikationsdesign hatte insofern die Rolle einer Jury für die Auswahl des Architekten. Andererseits war Audi die Architektur offenbar besonders wichtig.

Keller / I also mean it like that. At least, as far as the willingness to get involved in an experiment is concerned. This was noticeable from the start. And one more thing, if you can handle so much praise from my mouth: in contrast to most of your colleagues, you had done research and were informed about the current products of Audi.

Was this the decisive criterion?

Keller / No, but it was a good omen. Of course, we did not yet know what the architectural solution would look like. And even as he competed against four other agencies for the final decision in Ingolstadt, it was not yet clear what the outcome would be, if we worked together.

Ingenhoven / Because of the type of selection process, it was also not possible to test the cooperation.

Keller / Which was quite daring. During the two months prior to the presenta-tion, we behaved very impartially—or more precisely: we kept in the background. This was not an easy task.

Ingenhoven / To this extent, communications design had the role of a jury for the selection of the architect. On the other hand, the architecture was obviously very important to Audi.

Keller / Uns auch! Die Zeiten, in denen der Architekt ein Haus oder einen Messestand baute und dann die Graphiker kamen, um die Inhalte an die Wände zu kleben, sind vorbei. Nach unserer Auffassung sollte am Ende nicht mehr unterscheidbar sein, welches Element von wem stammt.

War das eine neue Erkenntnis?

Keller / Nein, aber eine Weiterentwicklung. Unsere erste Arbeit für Audi hatte »ganz persönlich« geheißen. Das war 1997, zur vorangegangenen IAA. Das Motto entsprach der Grundidee einer unmittelbaren Kontaktaufnahme zwischen Marke und Kunde. So konnte zum Beispiel jeder Besucher seinen Namen auf einer der Wände einschreiben lassen und den Messestand dadurch gewissermaßen mitgestalten: So entstand das größte Gästebuch der Welt. Oder es gab ein System von Betreuern, die für einzelne Themen zuständig waren und spezifische Fragen der Besucher individuell beantworteten. Dieses Einladende, diese persönliche Ansprache sollte auch dieses Mal transportiert werden. Doch um Hausherr zu sein, braucht man ein Haus. Das hatte bis dahin gefehlt.

Wie kommt man zu einem gemeinsamen Konzept?

Ingenhoven / Für die Teilnahme am Wettbewerb hatten wir von KMS ein Briefing erhalten, aus dem zwei zentrale Anforderungen hervorgingen: Die Architektur sollte eine in sich geschlossene logische Welt schaffen, die eine formale Identität von Messe zu Messe stiftet. Und es sollte eine leichte, transparente Arbeit sein, letzten Endes ein Spiegelbild des Unternehmens.

Keller / To us as well! The days in which the architect would construct a building or an exhibition stand and then the graphic designers would come to paste the "contents" onto the walls are over. In our view, it should no longer be discernable in the end, which element derives from which contributor.

Was this a new discovery?

Keller / No, but a further development. Our first work for Audi had been called "very personal". This was in 1997, at the previous International Auto Show. The motto corresponded to the basic idea of an immediate contact between the product make and the customer. Thus, for example, every visitor was able to have their name inscribed on one of the walls and thus in a sense contribute to the design of the exhibition stand: this created the largest guest book in the world. Or there was a system of attendants, who were responsible for individual topics and who would individually answer specific questions on the part of visitors. This inviting gesture, this personal address was to be conveyed this time as well. But in order to be a host, you first need a house. This had been missing so far.

How do you arrive at a common plan?

Ingenhoven / For the participation at the competition, we had received a briefing from KMS, which stated two central requirements: the architecture was supposed to create a self-contained logical world that establishes a formal identity from one show to another. And it was supposed to be a light and transparent piece of work; in the end, a mirror image of the company.

Keller / Für viele zeigte es sich ja erstmals von einer noch unbekannten Seite. Audi hatte damals gerade viele Plätze gutgemacht und galt als attraktivster Europäer. Alles war neu, alles war möglich. Dafür wollten wir auch einen gestalterischen Ausdruck finden.

»Zukunft« hieß das Thema der IAA – nahe liegend angesichts des bevorstehenden Jahrtausendwechsels. Inwiefern spielte es bei Ihren Überlegungen eine Rolle?

Keller / Jedes Unternehmen stellt sich als zukunftsorientiert dar. Audi war in einer Situation, in der dies keine pauschale Positionierung war, sondern Offenheit tatsächlich das Bild prägte. Dadurch war auch eine klare Abgrenzung gegenüber den Mitbewerbern möglich: BMW zeigte sich in meiner Wahrnehmung sehr kühl, sportlich und metallisch; Mercedes präsentierte sich gesetzt, als Erfinder des Autos sozusagen. Audi dagegen war im Aufbruch, hatte sich vom alten Image des Audi 80 endgültig gelöst.

Keller / For many, the company showed itself from an unfamiliar side. Just at that time, Audi had moved up many positions and was considered the most attractive European car maker. Everything was new, anything was possible. And we wanted to express this in design.

The theme of the International Auto Show was entitled "future"—an obvious choice considering the approaching turn of the millennium. To what extent did it play a role in your considerations?

Keller / Every company presents itself as oriented toward the future. Audi was in a situation in which this was not an indiscriminate positioning, but where openness actually characterized the public image. This made possible a clear differentiation from the competitors: I perceived BMW as very cool, sporty and metallic; Mercedes presented itself as dignified, as the inventor of the automobile, so to speak. Audi, by contrast, was on the move, having separated itself from the old image of the Audi 80 for good.

Ingenhoven / Surveys show that most people rate Audi's models very highly in all relevant aspects of car manufacture—sportiness, engine construction, technology, safety, design and progressiveness—that is, at the same level as the other leading makes. With regard to prestige, however, Audi nevertheless slips a little in the surveys. This is an interesting phenomenon.

So, after all, there is still the old association with the guy in suspenders.

Ingenhoven / Aus Umfragen geht hervor, dass die meisten die Modelle von Audi in allen relevanten Aspekten des Automobilbaus – Sportlichkeit, Motoren-konstruktion, Technik, Sicherheit, Design und Fortschrittlichkeit – sehr hoch, das heißt gleichauf mit den anderen Spitzenmarken, einschätzen. Beim Prestige allerdings rutscht Audi in den Umfragen trotzdem ein wenig ab. Das ist ein interessantes Phänomen.

Also doch noch das alte Hosenträger-Image?

Ingenhoven / Ein solches Image kann man offenbar nicht so schnell loswerden. Einzelne Markeneigenschaften – eine neue Keramikbremse oder eine Leicht-metall-Konstruktion – lassen sich schnell transportieren. Aber eine Markeniden-tität langfristig zu etablieren ist schwieriger. Deswegen haben wir unsere Auf-gabe so verstanden, eine Welt für Audi zu entwerfen, in der emotionale Marken-werte eine größere Präsenz, einen stärkeren visuellen Ausdruck bekommen als bisher.

Ist das nicht gerade die Aufgabe der Designer?

Ingenhoven / Architektur hat gute Chancen, Emotionalität zu transportieren. Eine gotische Kathedrale tut dies, indem sie den Besucher mit ihrer grandiosen Räumlichkeit umfängt. Gleichzeitig haben wir uns entschieden, das Thema Konstruktion anzugehen. Zwar wollten wir eine Welt schaffen, die die Gefühle anspricht – aber wir wollten sie mit den rationalen und technischen Mitteln des Ingenieurs entwerfen, die wiederum dem klassischen Markenkern von Audi entsprechen.

Ingenhoven / It obviously takes a long time to shed such an image. Individual brand characteristics—new ceramic brakes or a light alloy construction—can be conveyed quickly. But to establish a lasting identity of a make is more difficult. This is why we understood our task as one of designing a world for Audi, in which the emotional values of the make have a greater presence and gain a more powerful visual expression than has been the case to date.

Is this not precisely the task of designers?

Ingenhoven / Architecture is well suited for conveying emotionality. A Gothic cathedral does this by enveloping the visitor with its grandiose spatiality. At the same time, we decided to tackle the topic of construction. It is true that we wanted to create a world that speaks to feelings—but we wanted to design it with the rational and technical means of engineers, which in turn correspond to the classical core of the Audi make.

Keller / Technology was definitely an important keyword. And the products displayed were technologically very highly developed—not only the vehicles, but also the 'loop'.

Ingenhoven / As free as the 'loop' may appear, it is not an arbitrary form, which somehow has been made to stand upright. The flowing three-dimensionality is 100 percent classical engineering and not something merely dreamt up by means of a computer and then constructed from papier mâché. We are dealing a lot with engineers all over the world. They are not only familiar with Audi, but they also know the slogan "advancement through technology"—even in German.

Keller / Technik war auf jeden Fall ein wichtiges Stichwort. Es wurden ja auch technisch sehr ausgereifte Produkte gezeigt – nicht nur die Fahrzeuge, sondern eben auch der ›Loop‹.

Ingenhoven / So frei der ›Loop‹ auch aussieht, es ist keine willkürliche Form, die man irgendwie zum Stehen gebracht hat. Die fließende Dreidimensionalität ist zu 100 Prozent klassische Ingenieursarbeit und nicht nur mit dem Computer herbeigewünscht und am Ende aus Pappmaché gebaut. Wir haben viel mit Ingenieuren in aller Welt zu tun. Die kennen nicht nur Audi, sondern auch den Slogan »Vorsprung durch Technik« – sogar auf Deutsch.

Keller / Und dann gibt es noch die so genannten Markenwerte. Bei Audi lauten sie: »visionär«, »menschlich«, »leidenschaftlich« und »führend«, und nun werden Sie vielleicht sagen, ich soll aufhören mit dem werblichen Quatsch. So habe ich vorher auch darüber gedacht. Doch wenn man sie als vorgegebene Identitäts-merkmale ansieht, helfen sie einem – ungefähr so wie die Angaben in einem Rezept. Die Gewichtsangaben in Gramm haben noch wenig mit dem Genuss zu tun, es muss jemand auch noch vom Kochen was verstehen. Aber sie geben die Gewähr, an jedem Ort der Welt dasselbe Gericht kochen zu können. Und das heißt: dasselbe Gefühl auslösen zu können. Letzten Endes ist ja das Erleb-nis, das man sich mit dem Auto wünscht, der eigentliche Grund, es zu kaufen.

Keller / And then there are the so-called brand values. At Audi, these are called: "visionary", "human", "passionate" and "leading". And now you are perhaps going to tell me to stop with this advertising nonsense. That is what I used to think as well. Yet, if you regard these terms as pre-defined character traits, they can be helpful—somewhat like the specifications in a recipe. The specifications of quantities in cooking do not yet have much to do with the enjoyment of the taste of the food. One in addition has to know something about cooking. Yet these specifications guarantee that the same dish can be prepared anywhere in the world. And this means that it is possible to trigger the same feeling. In the end, the real reason for buying a car is the experience one hopes to have with it.

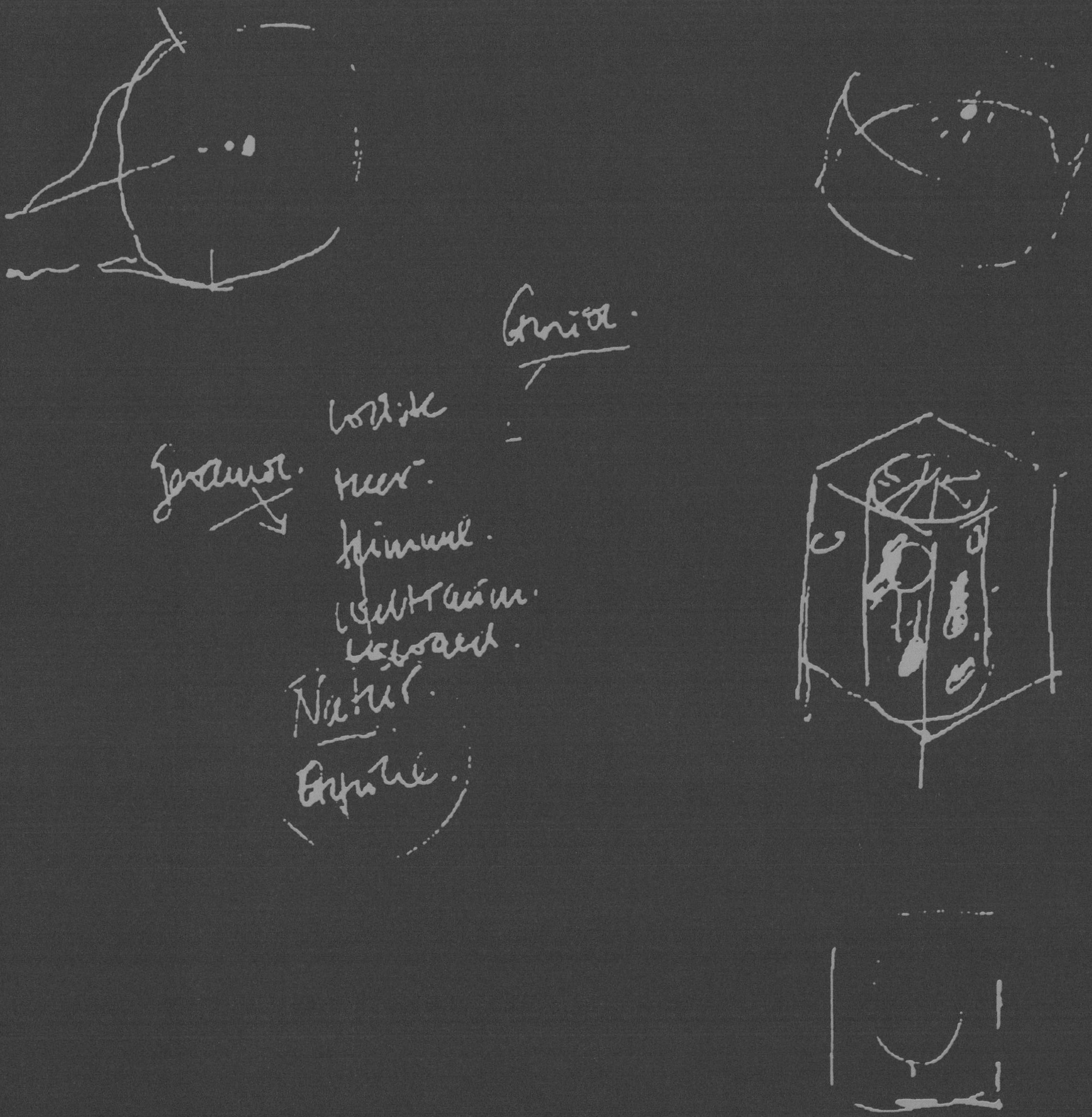
Wolke
Meer.
Himmel.
Weltraum.
Natur.

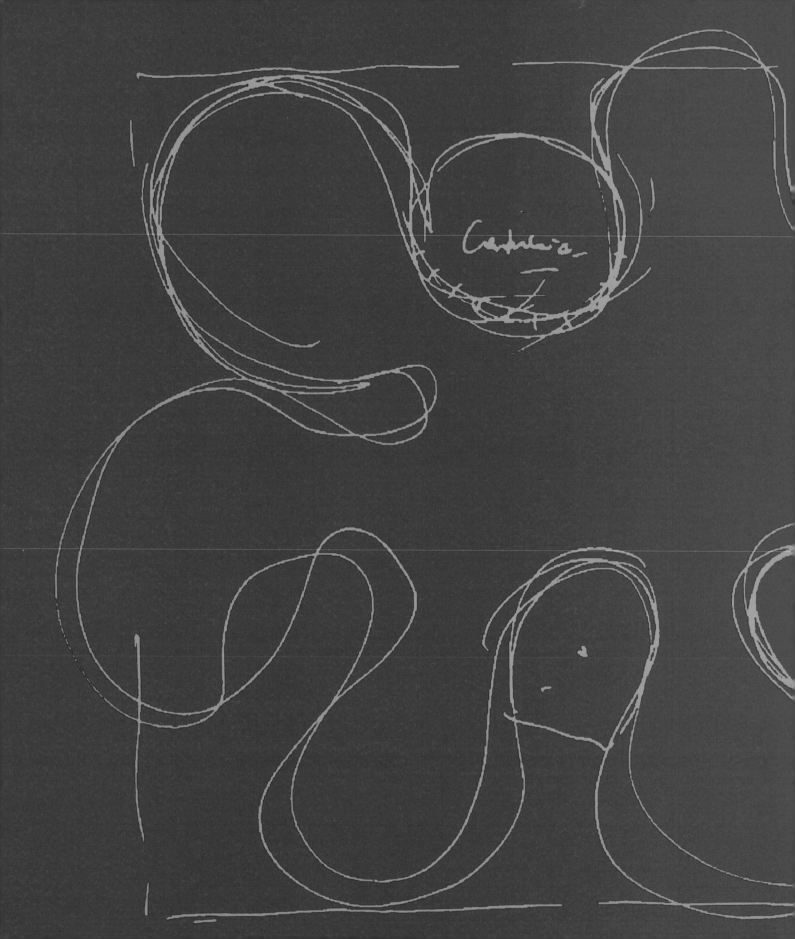

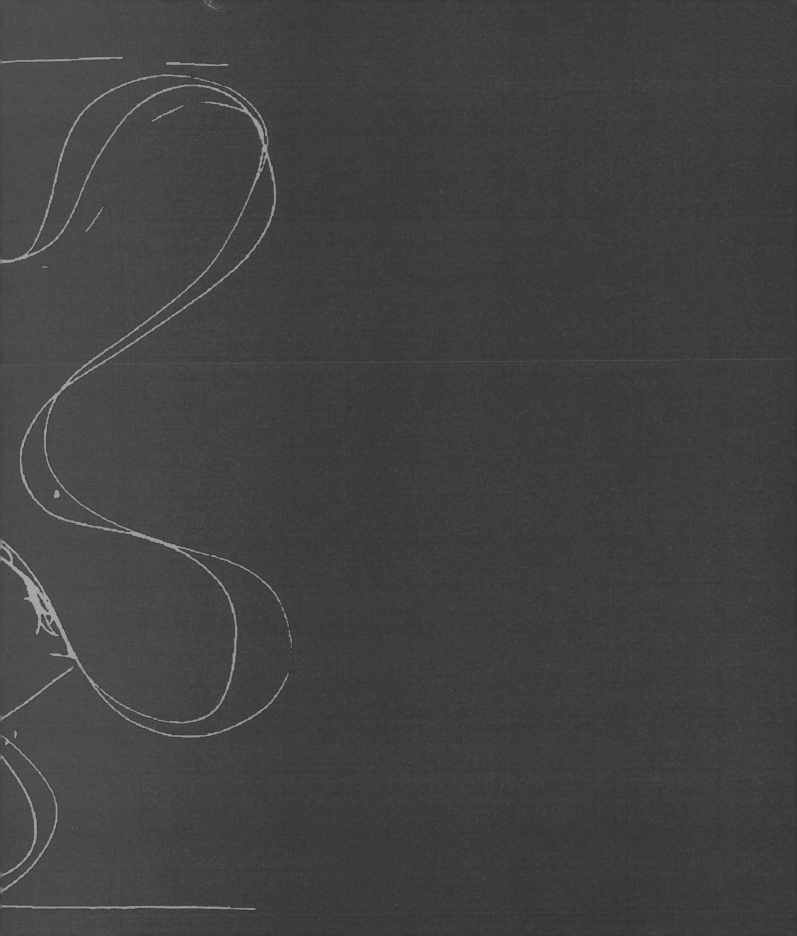

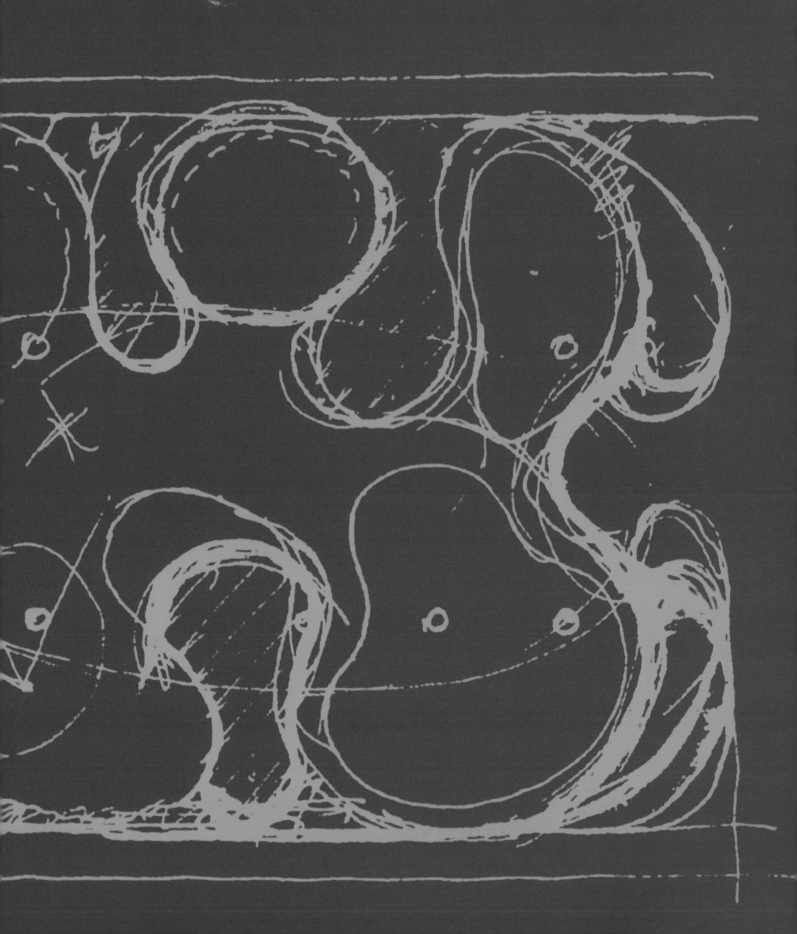

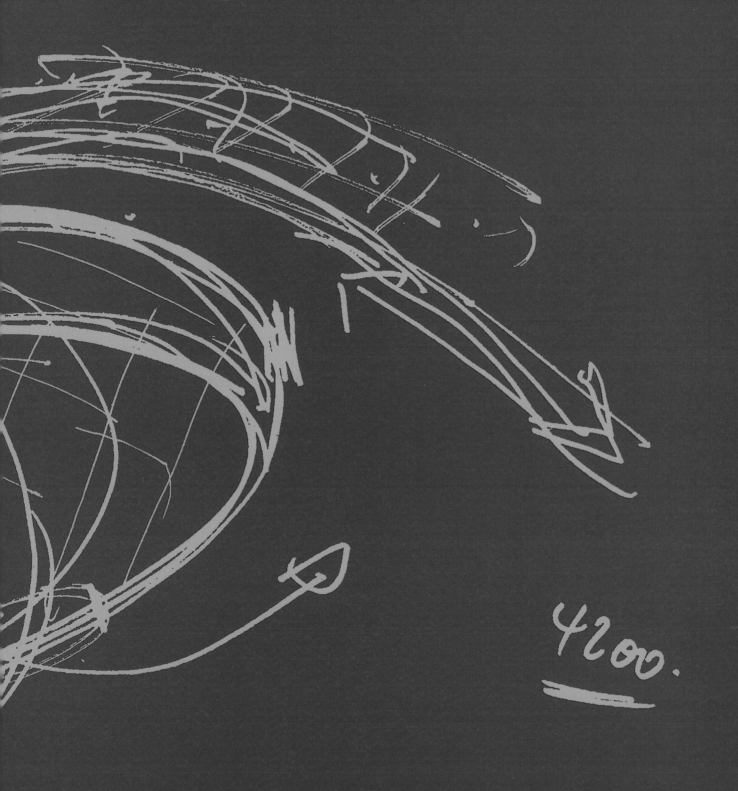

4200.

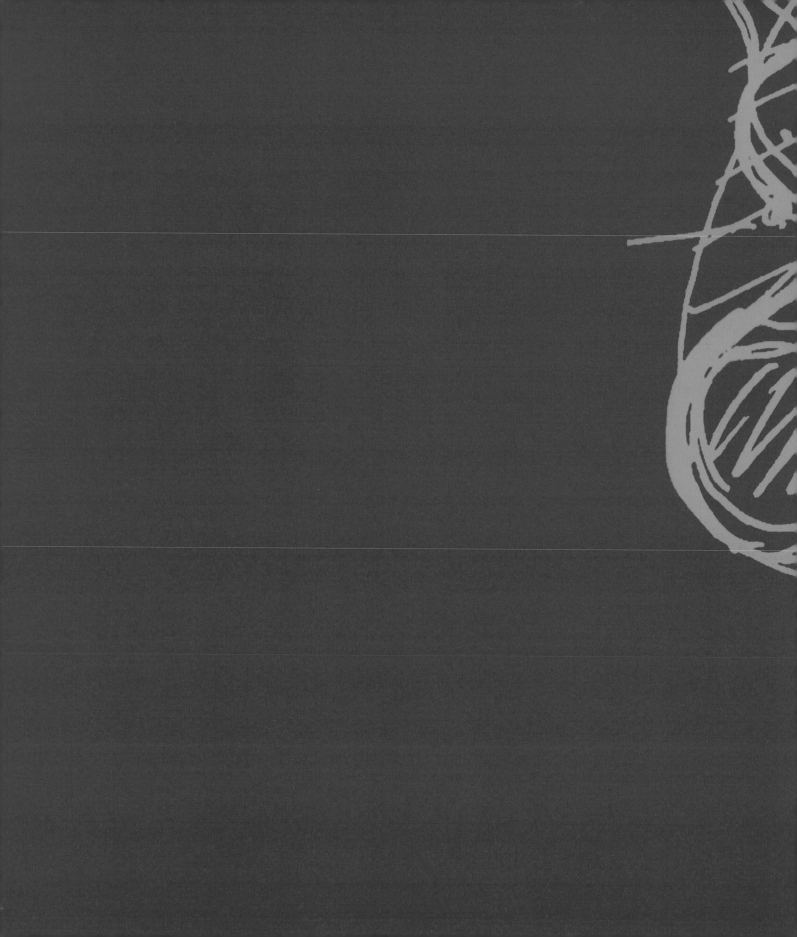

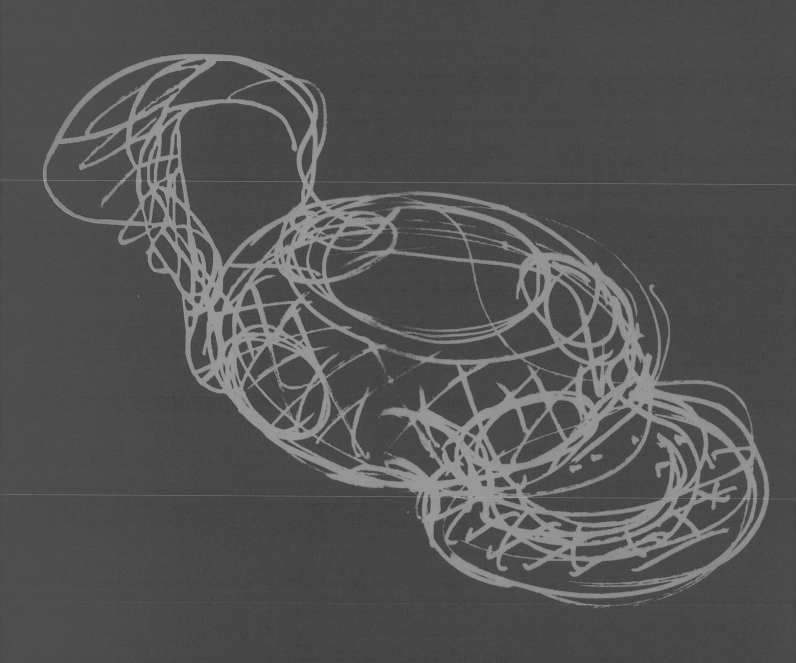

Wie kommt man mit diesen Vorgaben auf die Konstruktion des ›Loop‹?

Ingenhoven / Ausgangspunkt war der Gedanke, eine Welt zu schaffen. Darunter stelle ich mir immer etwas Umhüllendes, etwas Geschlossenes vor. Im Mutterleib. Unter Wasser. Oder wenn ich in einem Weizenfeld liege und die Ähren über mir zusammenfallen. Es gibt ein Kontinuum der Oberflächen, die Dimensionen haben fließende Übergänge. Aus diesen Überlegungen entstand eine simple Skizze, eine amöbenähnliche Form, die bereits viele entscheidende Aspekte beinhaltete.

Inwiefern?

Ingenhoven / Die Übertragung der Wölbung auf den Aufriss rief die gewünschte umhüllende Wirkung hervor. Außerdem ergab sich durch die Krümmungen eine frei stehende Konstruktion. Und: Die Ausbuchtungen boten sich für die Unterbringung verschiedener Schwerpunkte an, zum Beispiel einzelner Modell-Linien, zwischen denen es ebenfalls fließende Übergänge geben würde. So hatten wir bereits einen sehr flexiblen Grundriss für die Anforderungen verschiedener Messestände.

Keller / Mit dem Begriff »Messestand« sind wir übrigens beide gar nicht glücklich.

Ingenhoven / Das klingt danach, als sei alles genagelt, zusammengetackert und gerade mal ein bisschen überstrichen. So sehen Messestände eben oft auch aus.

Ihre Vorstellung von Messearchitektur ist offensichtlich eine andere.

How do you get from these guidelines to the construction of the 'loop'?

Ingenhoven / The starting point was the idea of creating a world. A world, I always imagine as something enveloping, something closed. In the womb. Under water. Or when I'm lying in a field of wheat and the ears close up above me. There is a continuum of surfaces. The dimensions have no clear-cut dividing lines. These considerations gave rise to a simple sketch, an amoebic form, which already contained many crucial aspects.

In what way?

Ingenhoven / The transfer of the curvature onto the elevation created the desired enveloping effect. Moreover, the curvatures resulted in a freestanding structure. And the indentations were suitable for accommodating various focal points such as individual model lines, for example, between which there would likewise be no sharp dividing lines. Thus, we already had a very flexible layout for the requirements of various exhibition stands.

Keller / By the way, neither of us is at all happy with the term "exhibition stand".

Ingenhoven / It sounds as if everything is nailed or tacked together and barely painted over. And this is what exhibition stands often look like.

You obviously have a different idea of trade show architecture.

Ingenhoven / Ja. Wir haben das Projekt unter anderem als große Chance zum Experimentieren begriffen, frei von allen Zwängen des Hausbaus, von bauphysikalischen Fragen, von Energiebilanzen und anderen konstruktiven Einengungen.

Dafür mussten Sie mit den spezifischen Messerscheinungen zurechtkommen…

Ingenhoven / Die Bedingungen in der Messehalle waren eher mau. Lassen Sie einmal so eine Halle im ›rohen‹ Zustand auf sich wirken – nicht eben inspirierend. Noch dazu lief in Frankfurt der Hauptdurchgang für die Besucher mitten durch die 5000 Quadratmeter große Audi-Fläche. Uns war wichtig, dass die entworfene Welt auf jeden Fall als Ganzes wahrgenommen und durch solche Vorgaben nicht zerteilt wurde. Die Messebedingungen verlangten erst recht eine Konstruktion ohne Innen und Außen, zumindest nicht in dem Sinne, dass es eine attraktive und eine schmucklose Seite gibt. Eine Konstruktion, die ohne Abstützung, ohne Verkleidung, ohne Verblendung auskommt.

Keller / Das war ein bestechender Aspekt des Entwurfs, der dem Begriff der Transparenz eine zusätzliche Dimension gab und genau mit unserem Ansatz zusammentraf. Alle Bereiche waren gleichberechtigt, dadurch ergab sich eine ideale Balance von Markenkommunikation und Produktinformation.

Ingenhoven / Auf jeder Messe gibt es Bedarf an Facilities und abgeschlossenen Räumen in erheblichem Umfang – Lounges, Büros, Küchen, Besprechungsräume, Garderoben. Dafür braucht man Flächen, die in unterschiedlichem Maße dem Blick des Publikums entzogen sind. Deswegen war es wichtig, eine Form zu finden, die sozusagen positiv und negativ funktioniert. Auf der einen Seite bietet sie einen perfekten Auftritt für die Autos. Auf der Rückseite, die aber nicht als solche erscheint, erlaubt sie immer noch, ansprechende Räume zu bauen.

Ingenhoven / Yes. We took this project, among other things, as a great opportunity for experimenting, free of all the constraints of house construction, of considerations from the perspective of building physics, of energy balances and other constructional restrictions.

Instead, you had to deal with specific trade show phenomena…

Ingenhoven / The conditions in the exhibition hall were rather bad. Try to take in the effect of such a hall in its 'raw' state—not exactly inspiring. On top of it, in Frankfurt, the main passageway for the visitors ran right through the 5000 square meter Audi area. For us it was important that the designed world be perceived as a whole and not be divided through this general set-up. The trade show conditions especially demanded a construction without an inside and an outside, at least not in the sense of there being an attractive and a plain side. We needed a construction that would work without supports, without paneling, without facing.

Keller / This was a fascinating aspect of the design, which gave an additional dimension to the concept of transparency, and which matched perfectly with our approach. All areas were given equal weight, thus providing for an ideal balance between brand communication and product information.

Ingenhoven / At any trade show there is a considerable need for facilities and enclosed spaces—lounges, offices, kitchens, conference rooms, check-rooms. For this purpose, you need areas that are to varying degrees removed from public view. This is why it was important to find a form that functions, so to speak, both positively and negatively. On the positive side, this form offers a perfect stage for the cars. On the backside—which, however, must not appear as such—it still offers the opportunity for building appealing rooms.

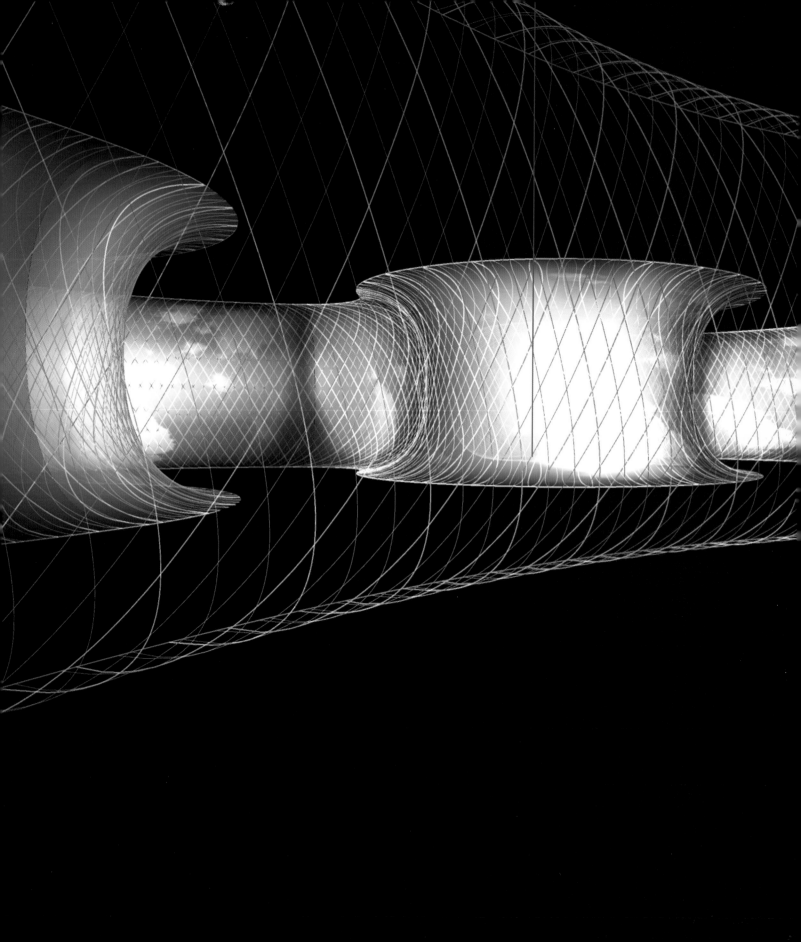

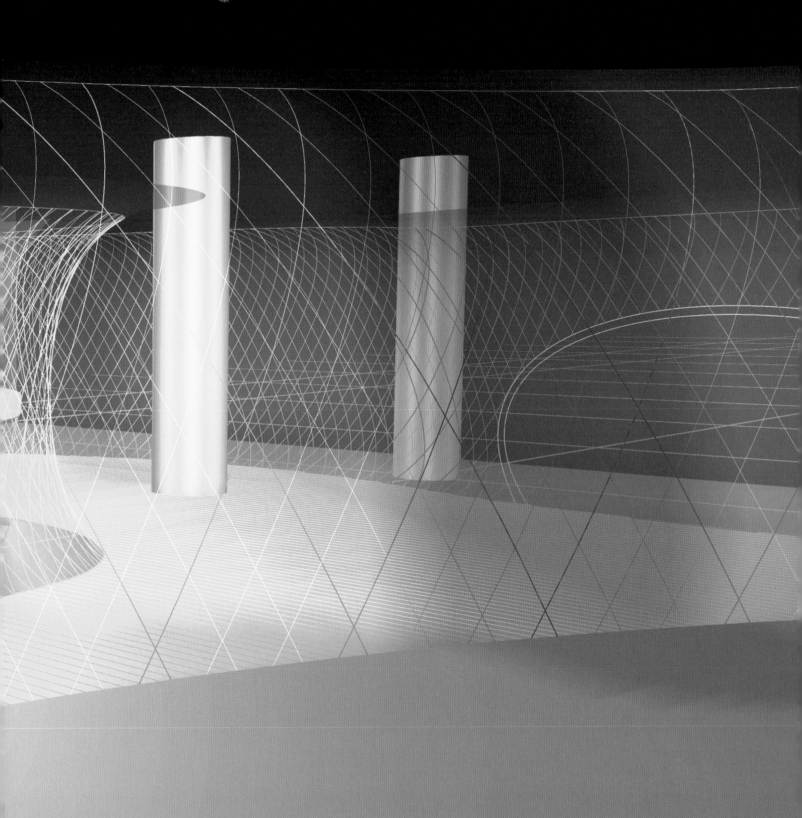

NAPIER UNIVERSITY L.I.S.

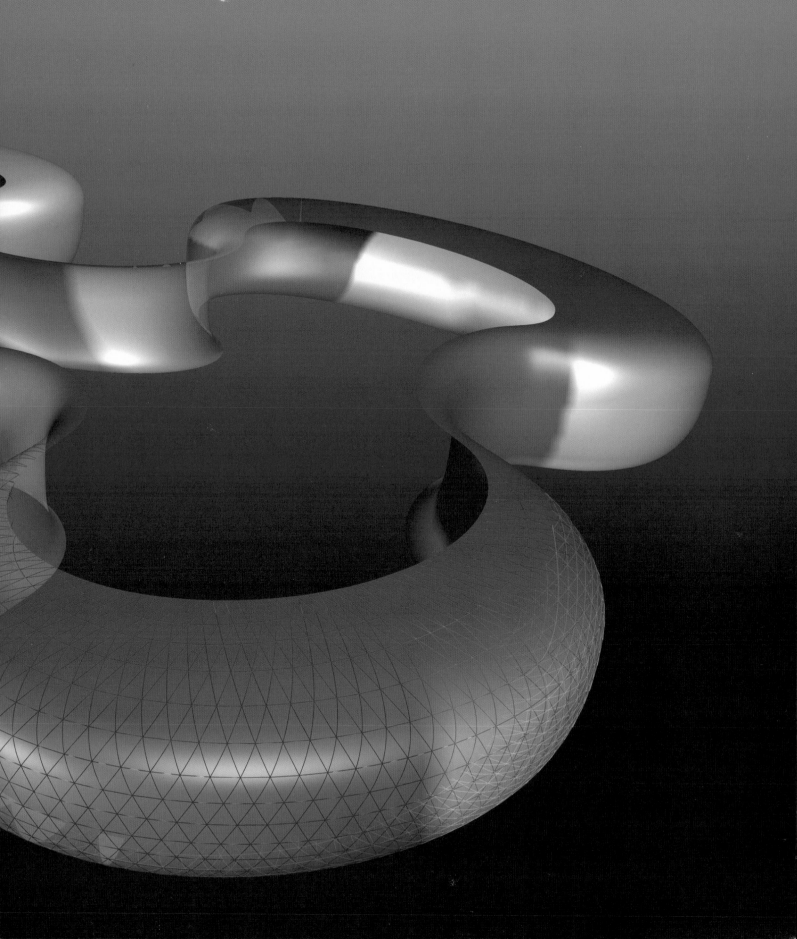

Montagereihenfolge:

1) Aufbau des Messestandbodens aus elementierten Holztafeln

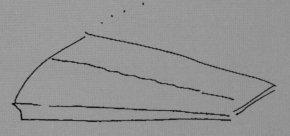

2. Aufbau eines verschiebbaren Gerüstes für Montage Kohlefasernohre und später die Glaselemente ca 10 m breit

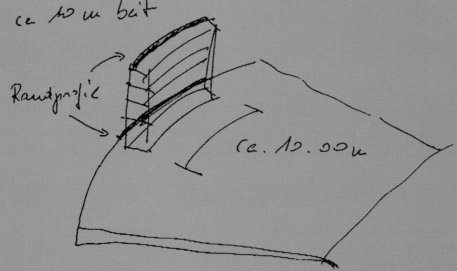

Randprofil

ce. 10.00 u

Fixierung der oberen und unteren Randabschlüsse
Einbau der Kohlefasernohre segmentweite ca 10.00 u

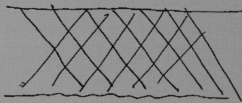

④

3) Komplementierung der Struktur

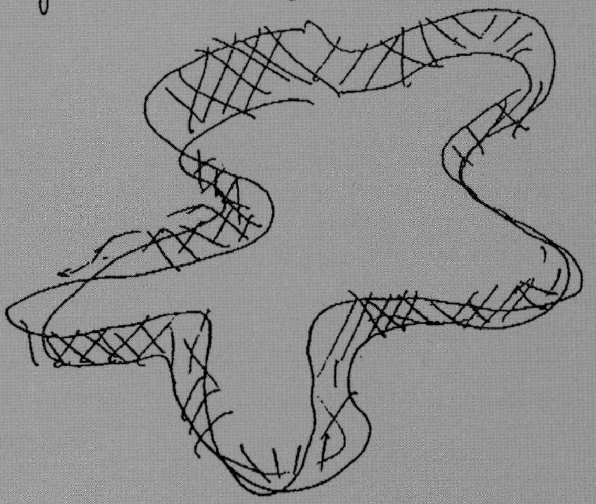

Stützgerüst fertig montiert

4)

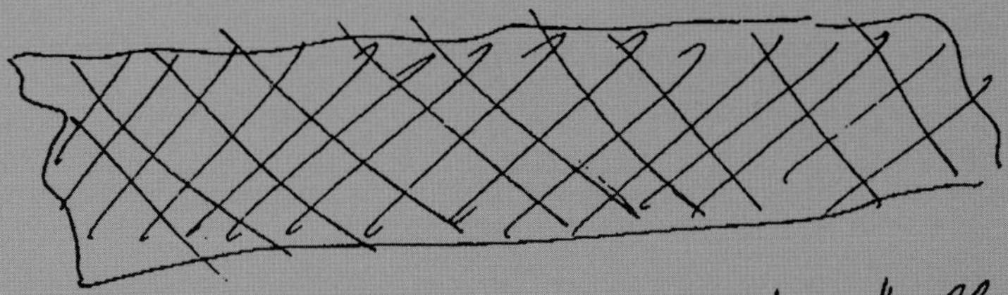

Auslegen des Kevlarnetzes auf den Abdeckleisten
Aufschrauben der Gußkunten ──────⟶

Verkürzung des Randes
Fixierung

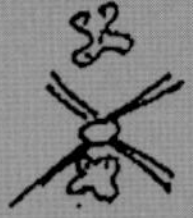

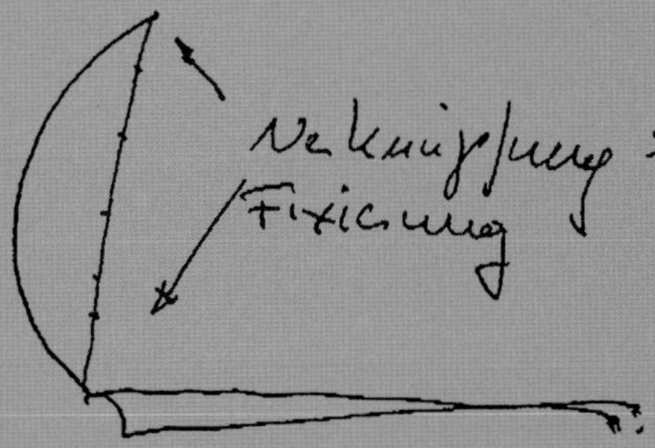

Neuspannen mit den Diagonalen am Tragegerüst
der Kohlefaserstäbe

⑤

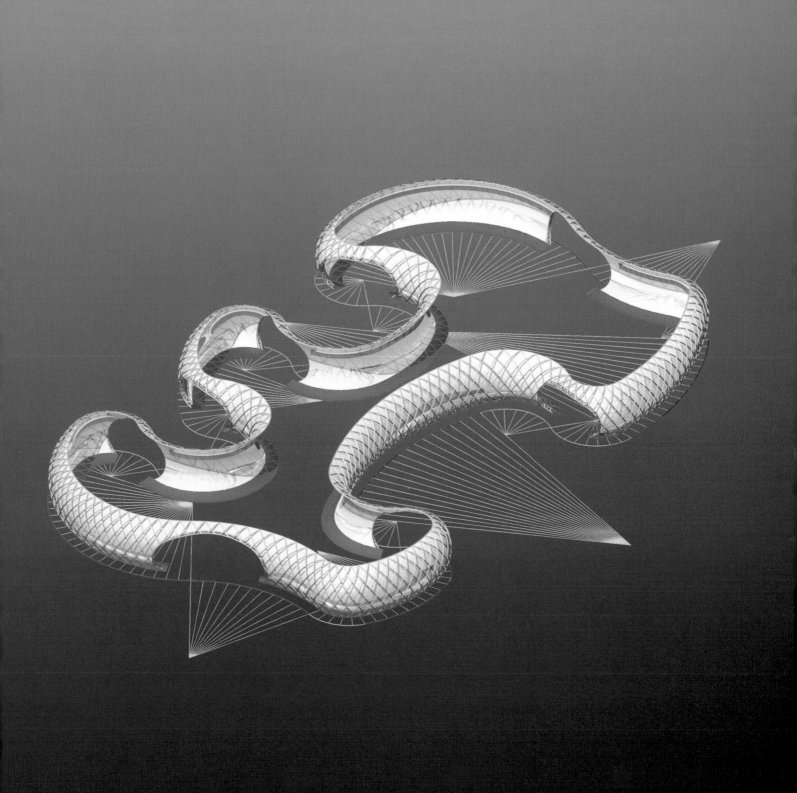

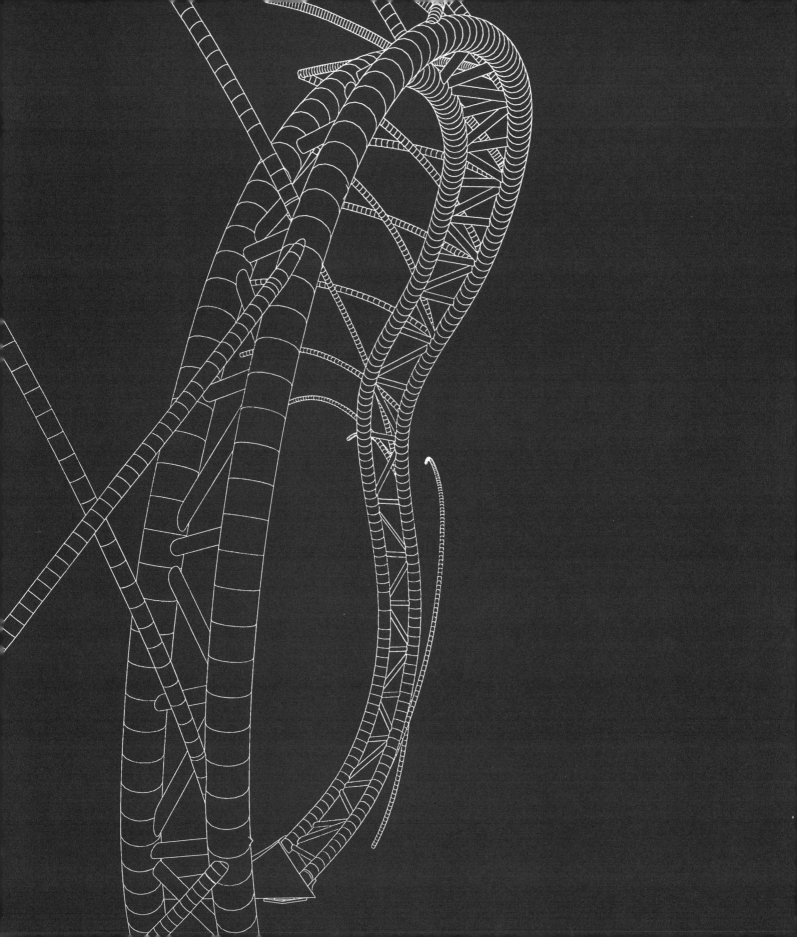

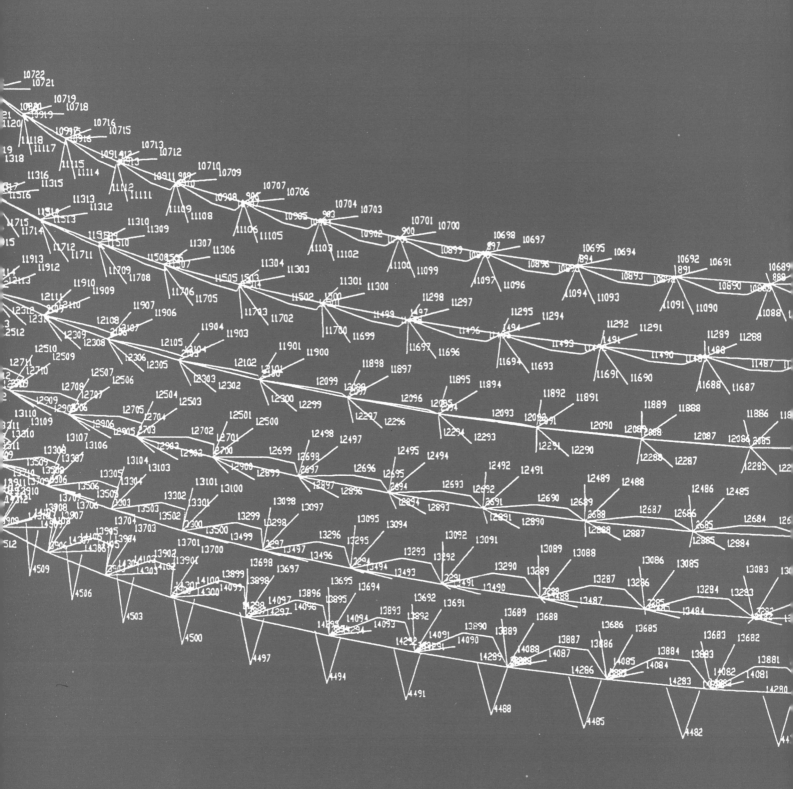

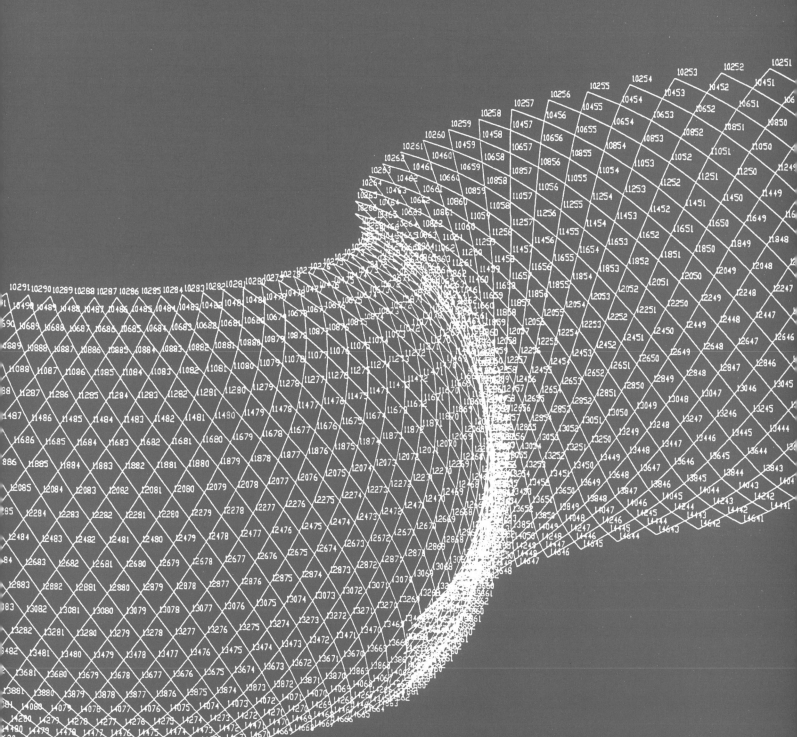

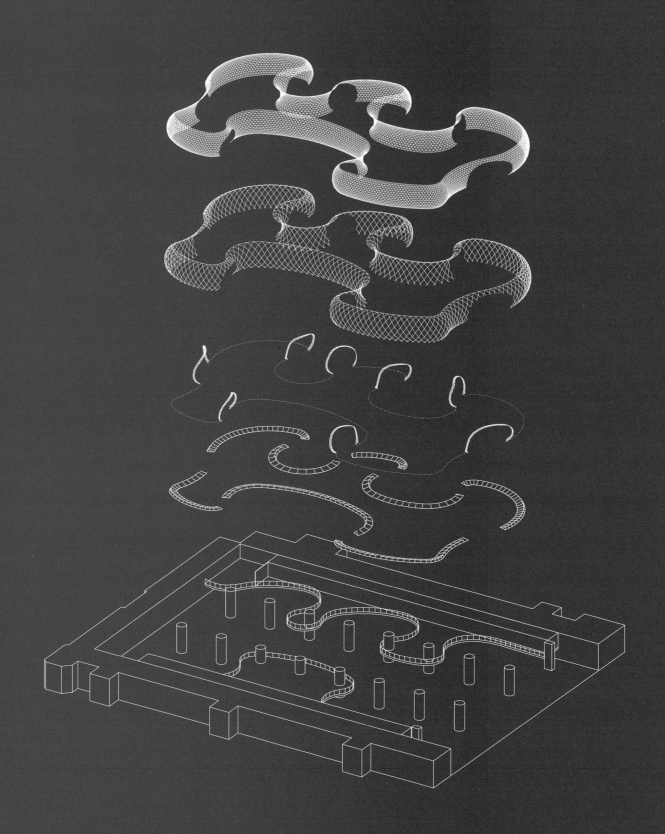

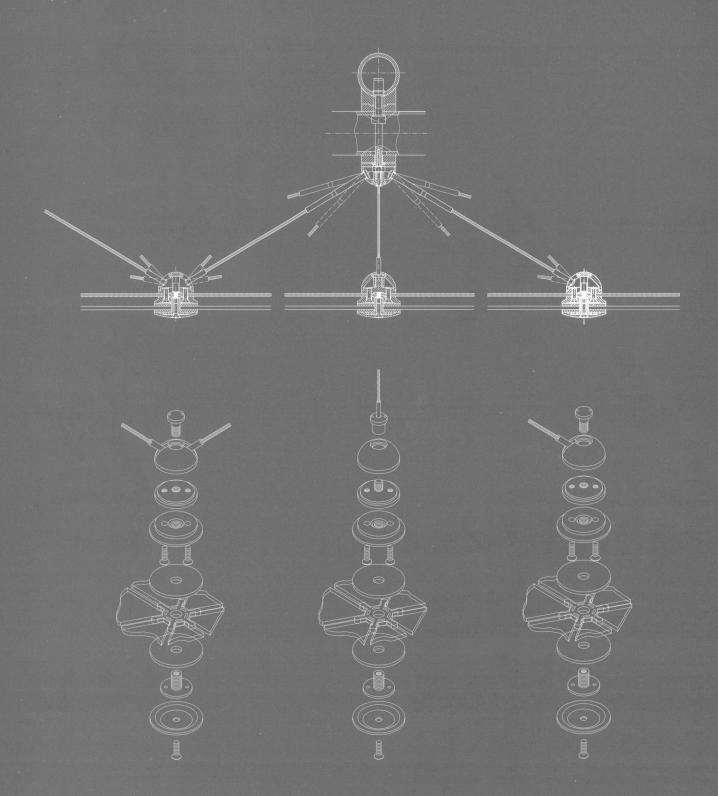

Für die Konstruktion haben Sie einen Spezialisten hinzugezogen.

Ingenhoven / Ja, den Tragwerksplaner Werner Sobek. Aus den gemeinsamen Überlegungen ist die Seilnetzkonstruktion des ›Loop‹ entstanden. Das primäre Tragsystem besteht aus miteinander verschraubten Stahlröhren, die ein dreidimensionales, rautenförmiges Grid bilden. Das ist in sich stabil – durch den doppelt gekrümmten Grundriss und die einfache Krümmung im Aufriss. Über die Kreuzungspunkte der Rohre wiederum sind Stahlseile verspannt, die ein feineres Netz mit dreieckigen Maschen bilden. Darin werden dreieckige Glasscheiben von etwa 50 cm Kantenlänge eingehängt.

Warum Dreiecke?

Ingenhoven / Gewölbte Oberflächen lassen sich bekanntlich durch Gitter aus Vielecken simulieren, und es war aus Kosten- und Produktionsgründen unerlässlich, plane Glasscheiben zu verwenden. Wir haben uns für die geometrisch einfachste Lösung entschieden, das Dreieck, und dabei eine Seitenlänge gewählt, die den Gesamteindruck der Rundung gewährleistete. Wir haben so schon insgesamt 12 000 Glasscheiben eingesetzt, darunter 2000 verschiedene Typen – der ›Loop‹ war schließlich sechs Meter hoch 360 Meter lang. Hätten wir die Polygonalität noch weiter treiben wollen, hätte der Wahnsinn Methode bekommen.

Wann wussten Sie, ob die Konstruktion funktioniert?

Ingenhoven / Jedenfalls noch nicht, als wir Werner Sobek baten, sie durchzurechnen. Später haben wir auch noch auf Wunsch von Audi in einer alten Werkhalle in Ingolstadt 20 Meter ›Loop‹ zur Probe aufgebaut. Da waren wir endgültig über den Berg.

For the construction itself, you called in a specialist.

Ingenhoven / Yes, the supporting framework designer Werner Sobek. The rope net construction of the 'loop' resulted from our joint deliberations. The primary support system consists of steel pipes that are screwed together to form a three-dimensional diamond-shaped grid. This is inherently sturdy—due to the double curved ground plan and the single curvature in the profile. Steel ropes are tied across the intersections of the pipes, forming a finer net with a triangular mesh. Triangular panes of glass of a side length of approximately 50 cm are hung into the mesh.

Why triangles?

Ingenhoven / As everybody knows, curved surfaces can be simulated through grids consisting of polygons. And for reasons of cost and manufacture, it was imperative to use flat panes of glass. We decided on the geometrically simplest solution of using triangles and choosing a side length that would guarantee the overall impression of a curvature. In this way, we already had to insert a total of 12,000 panes of glass of 2,000 different types—the 'loop', after all, is six meters high and 360 meters long. If we had taken polygonality even further, the madness would have gained method.

When did you know that the construction would work out?

Ingenhoven / Definitely not at the time we asked Werner Sobek to make the calculations for the construction. Later, at the request of Audi, we even built a 20 meter 'loop' for testing purposes in an old workshop in Ingolstadt. At that point, we were out of the woods for good.

Waren Sie sehr erleichtert?

Ingenhoven / Ich denke, der Auftraggeber war es noch mehr. Bei der Aussicht, dass es nicht funktionieren könnte, wird selbst der Experimentierfreudigste relativ ernst. Soll er dann schnell noch seinen alten Stand aufbauen, der irgendwo verstaubt herumliegt? Audi kann ja nicht einfach die IAA absagen.

Sie haben für den Autokonzern eine avancierte Konstruktion geplant, neue Formen ausprobiert und das Risiko nicht gescheut. Das Experiment selbst wird zur Entsprechung des Mottos »Fortschritt durch Technik«. Wie passt die Arbeit am ›Loop‹ zu Ihrem eigenen Architekturbüro?

Ingenhoven / Wir hatten ein Jahr davor, im Frühjahr 1998, den Wettbewerb für den Neubau des Stuttgarter Hauptbahnhofes gewonnen. Damals kamen gerade die Versuche in Mode, am Computer neue räumliche Phänomene zu generieren, seitdem wird viel von Raumkontinua, von Liquid Architecture, von Hybrid Forms gesprochen. Wir haben mit dem Stuttgarter Projekt unseren ersten Versuch in diese Richtung unternommen – aber auf eine völlig andere Art und Weise.

Was war anders?

Ingenhoven / Zusammen mit Frei Otto haben wir nicht eine beliebige Form erfunden, sondern eine völlig logische Konstruktion mit fließender Dreidimensionalität entworfen. Insofern war der Audi-Auftrag nicht nur ein Experiment für sich, sondern auch die Möglichkeit, die eigene Architektursprache mit Hilfe neuer Techniken weiterzuentwickeln.

Were you greatly relieved?

Ingenhoven / I think the client was even more relieved. At the prospect that a design might not work out, even those most enthusiastic about experimentation become relatively serious. Should they instead quickly assemble the old exhibition stand that is still lying around somewhere gathering dust? After all, Audi cannot simply cancel the International Auto Show.

You have planned an advanced construction for the automaker. You have tried out new forms and did not shy away from risk. The experiment itself becomes the appropriate response to the motto "advancement through technology". How does the work on the 'loop' fit with your own architectural firm?

Ingenhoven / One year earlier, in the spring of 1998, we had won the competition for the new construction of the Stuttgart central station. At that time, it was becoming fashionable to generate new spatial phenomena on computers. And since then there has been much talk of spatial continua, liquid architecture and hybrid forms. With the Stuttgart project, we made our first attempt in this direction—but in a completely different manner.

What was different?

Ingenhoven / Together with Frei Otto, we did not invent an arbitrary form, but rather designed a completely logical construction with a flowing three-dimensionality. To this extent, the Audi contract was not merely an isolated experiment, but also an opportunity to develop our own architectural language further by means of new techniques.

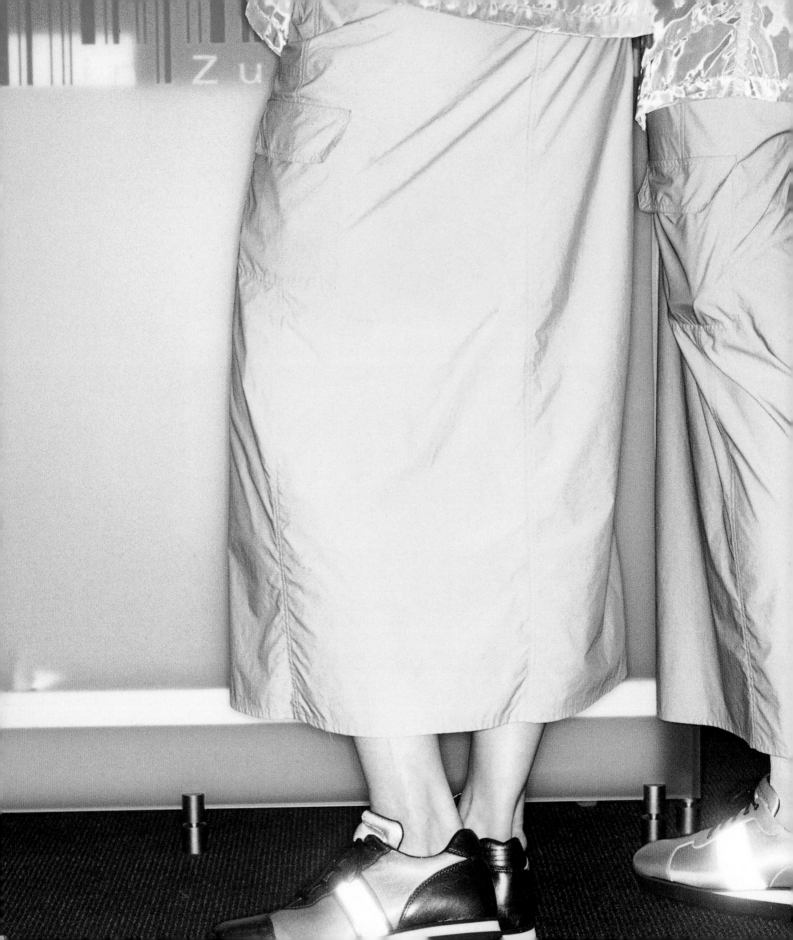

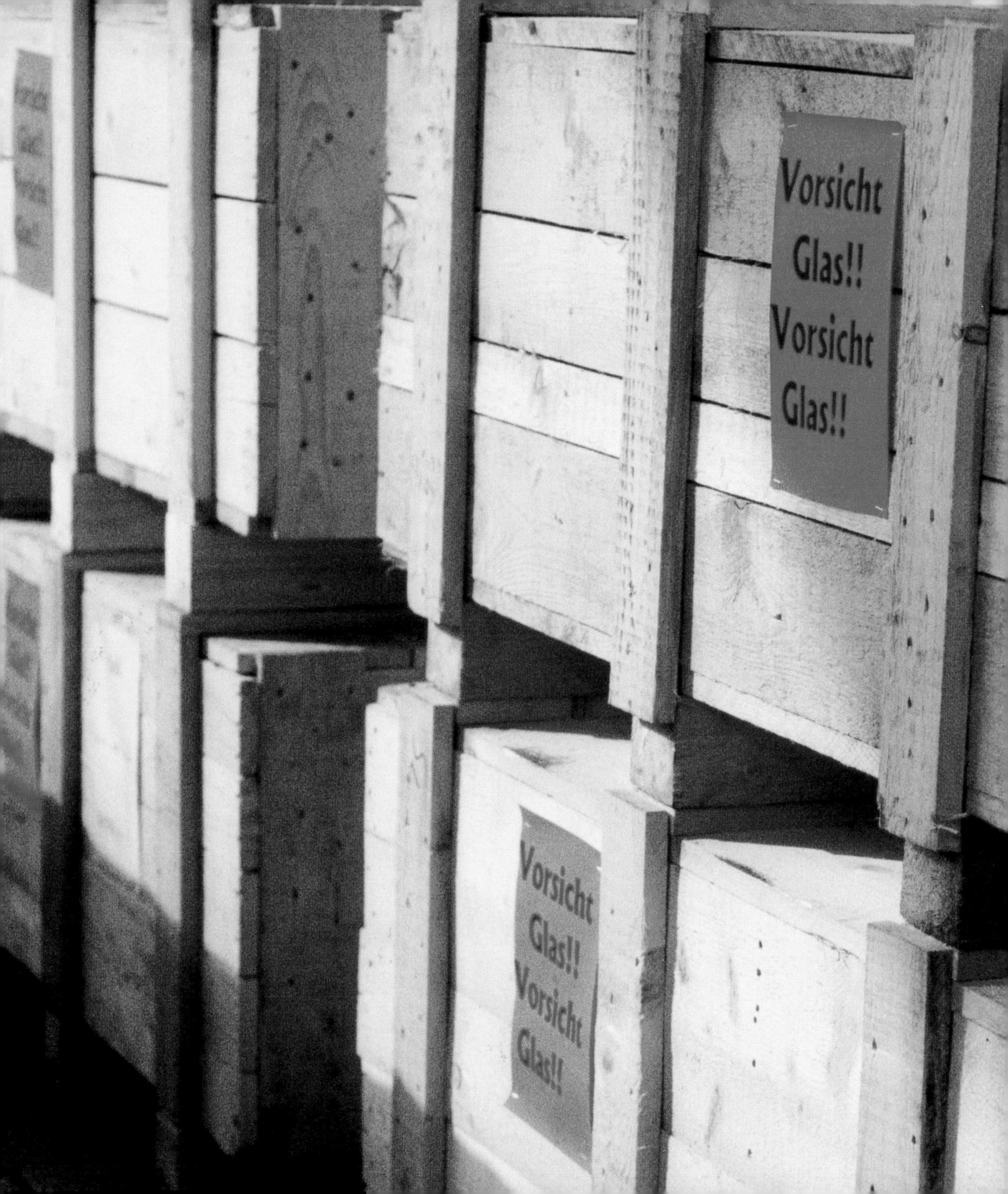
Vorsicht
Glas!!
Vorsicht
Glas!!
Vorsicht
Glas!!
Vorsicht
Glas!!

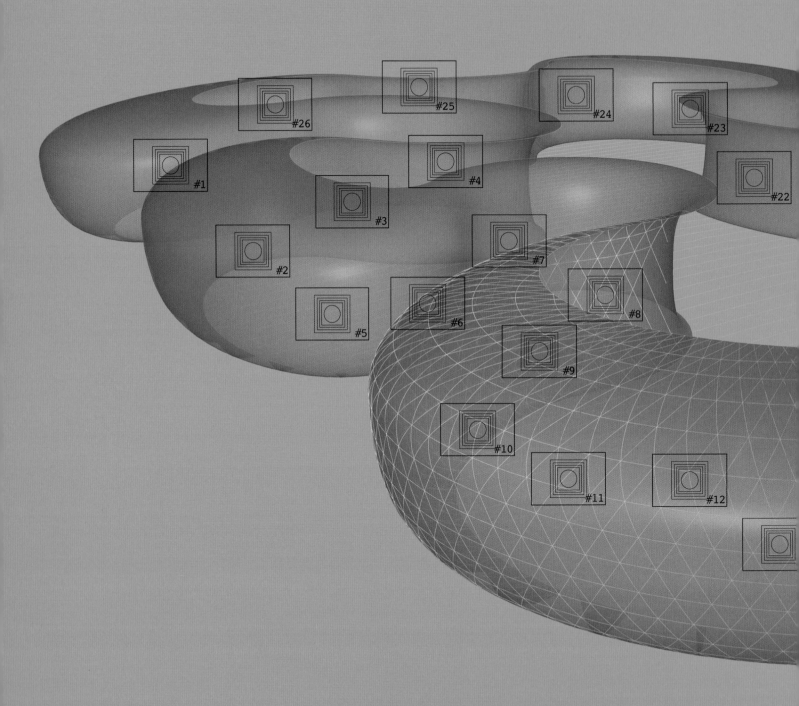

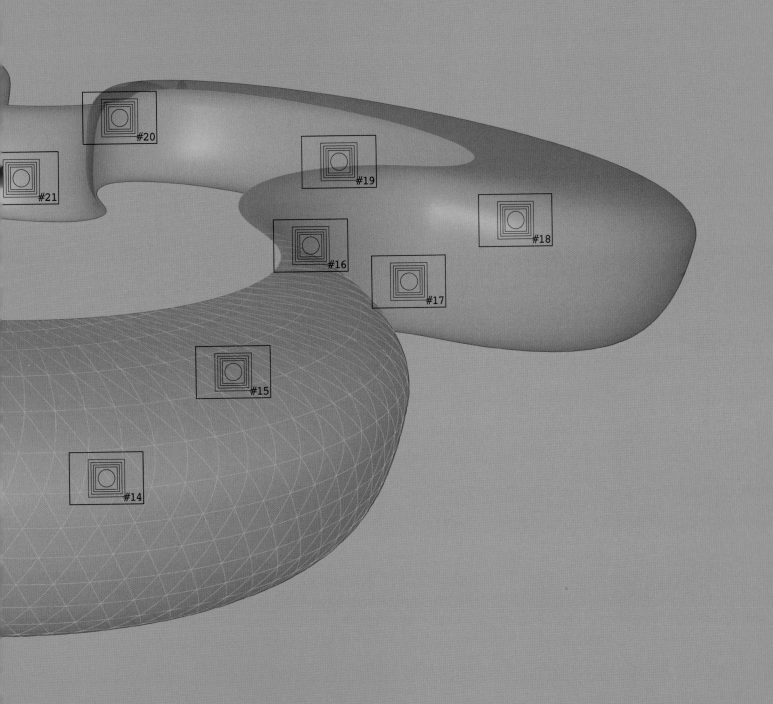

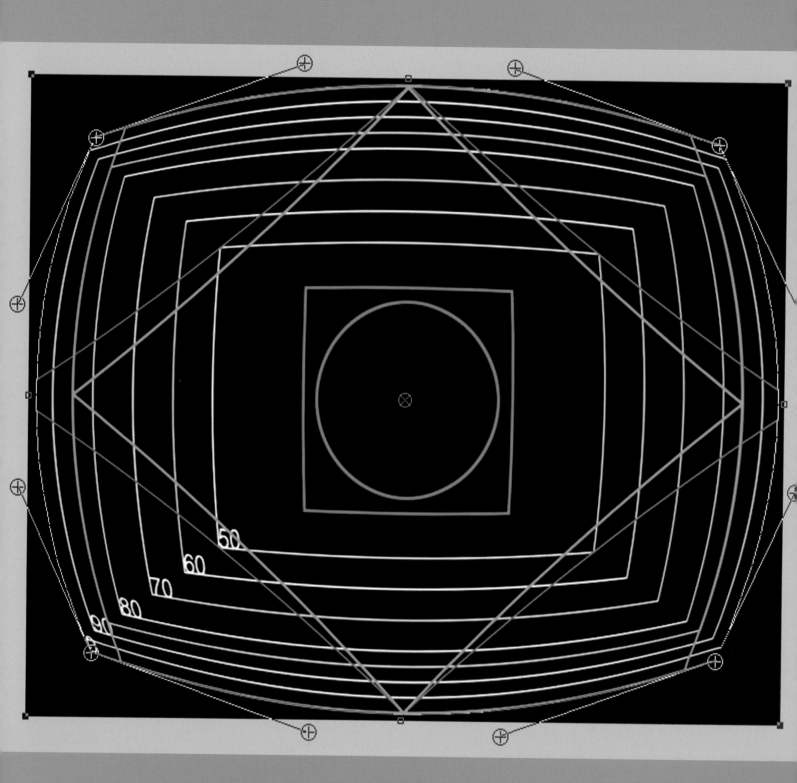

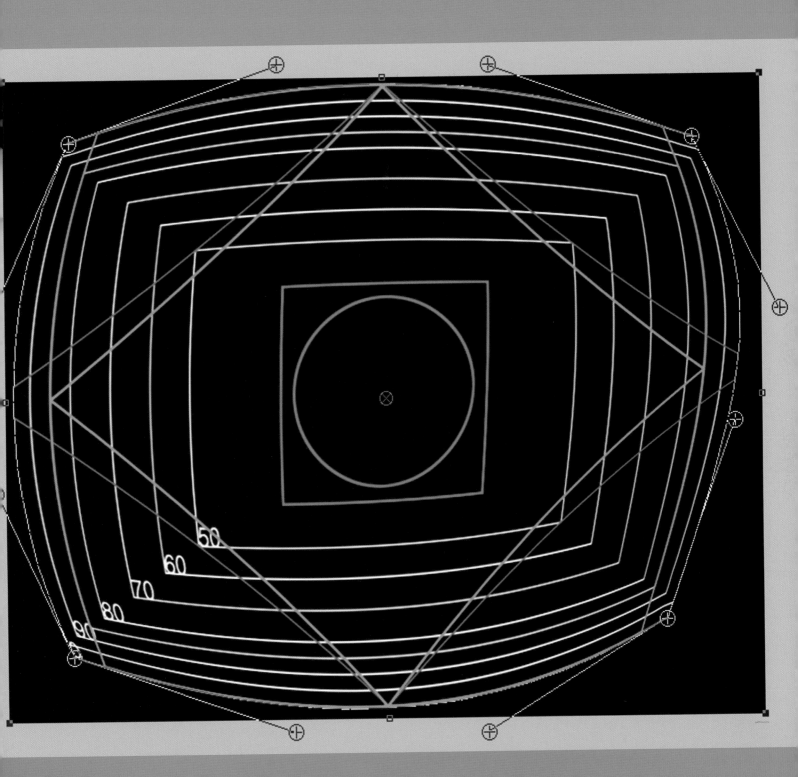

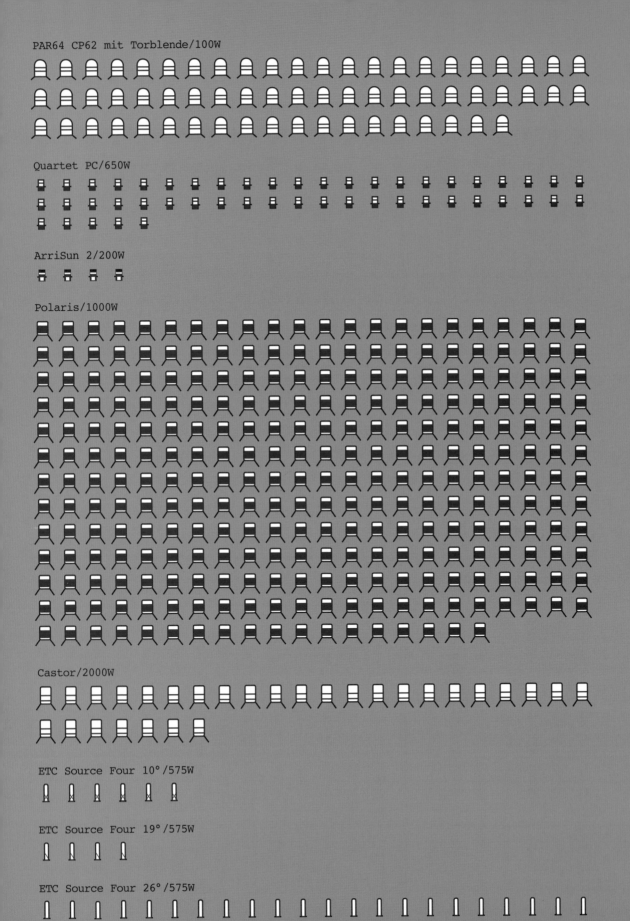

PAR64 CP62 mit Torblende/100W

Quartet PC/650W

ArriSun 2/200W

Polaris/1000W

Castor/2000W

ETC Source Four 10° /575W

ETC Source Four 19° /575W

ETC Source Four 26° /575W

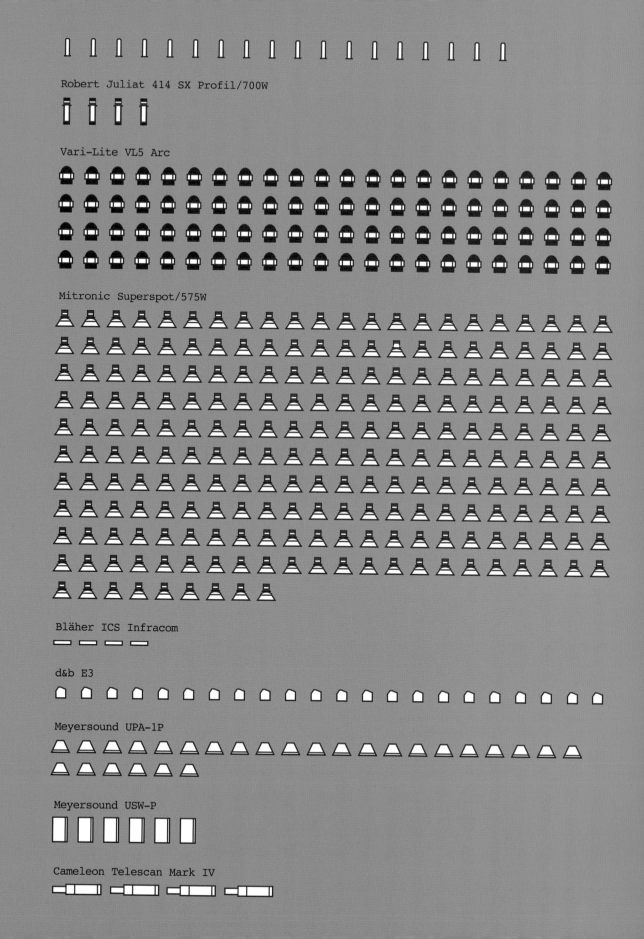

Robert Juliat 414 SX Profil/700W

Vari-Lite VL5 Arc

Mitronic Superspot/575W

Bläher ICS Infracom

d&b E3

Meyersound UPA-1P

Meyersound USW-P

Cameleon Telescan Mark IV

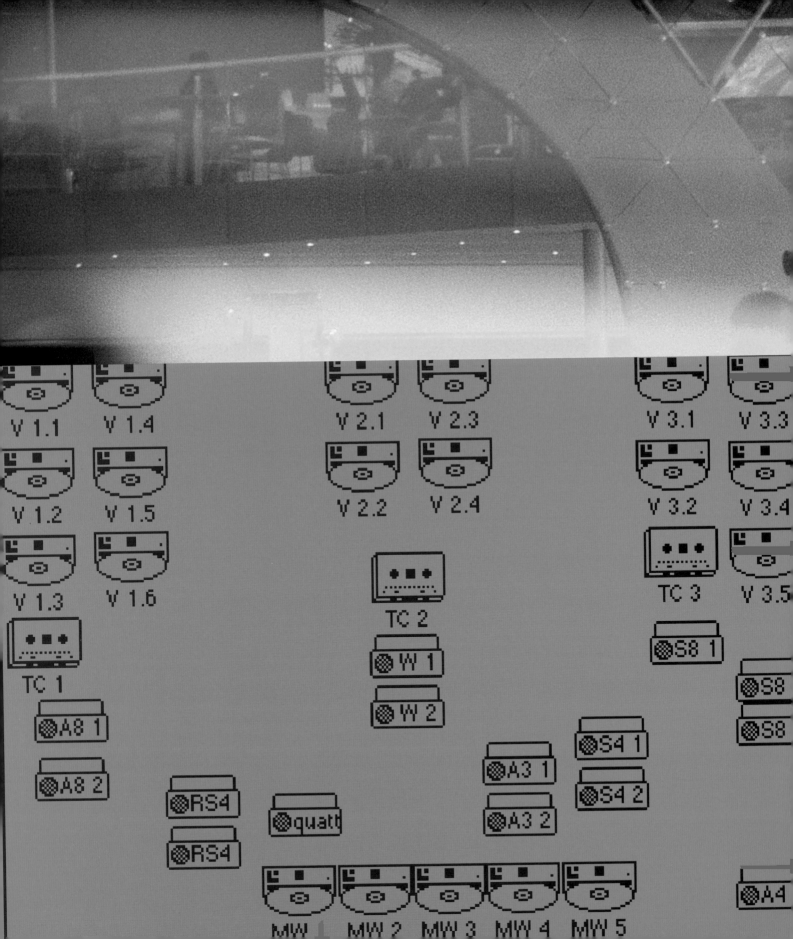

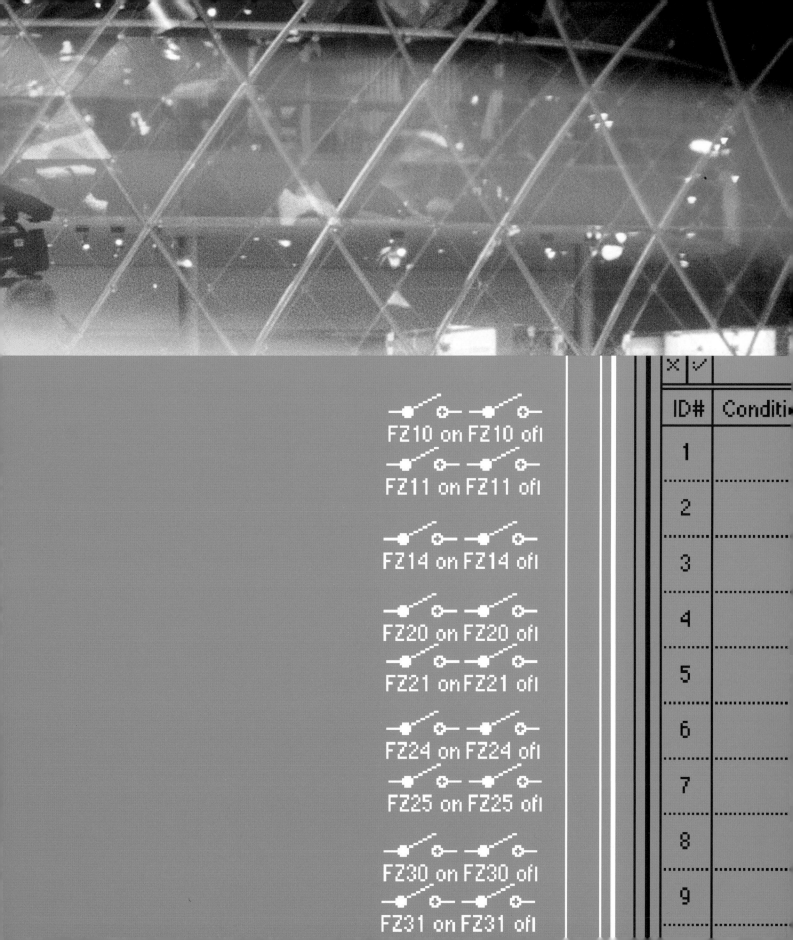

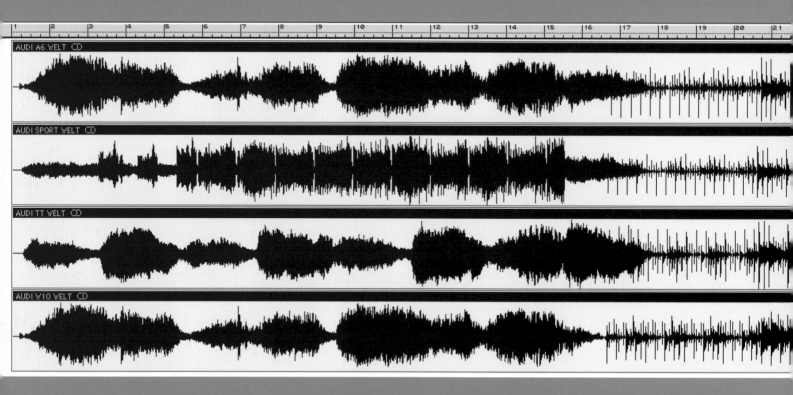

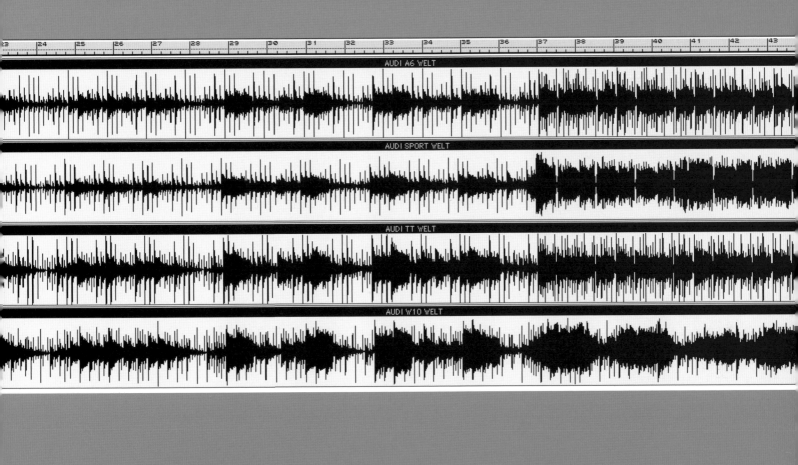

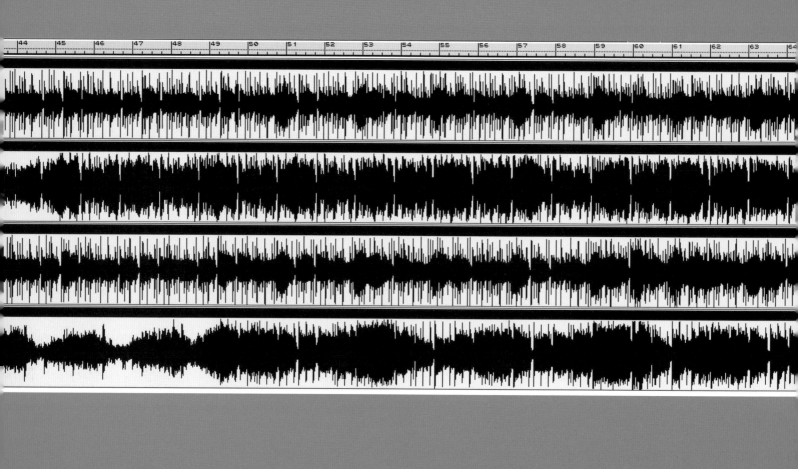

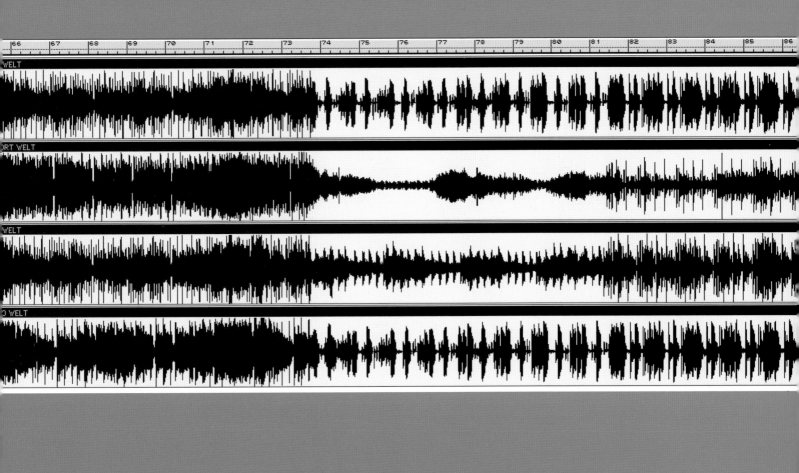

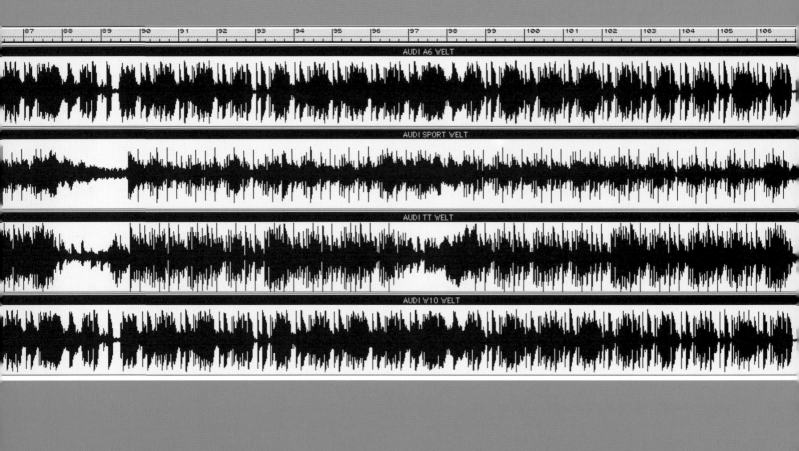

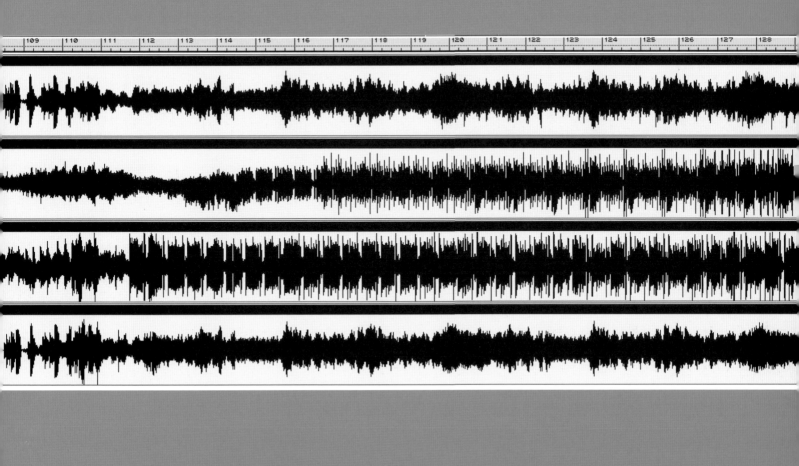

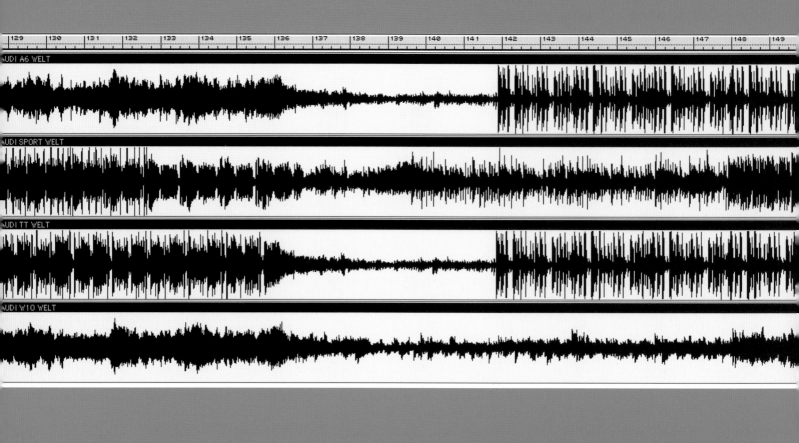

Zum Konzept gehörte nicht nur der ›Loop‹ als fließende und transparente Groß-
form, sondern auch die Idee, ihn großflächig zu bespielen. Wie waren die
Projektionen auf die rund 2000 Quadratmeter gekrümmten Glases angelegt?

Ingenhoven / Wir gingen von der Überlegung aus, dass die Besucher im Normalfall stunden-, manche auch tagelang auf der Messe sind. Sie sehen nichts
vom Tageslicht, es ist eine furchtbare Innenwelt, eine Black Box. Gegen diese
Eintönigkeit wollten wir eine Struktur setzen, einen Rhythmus: ziehende Wolken
zeigen, Sternenhimmel, Unterwasserbilder, Weizenfelder – bewegte Natur
also. Wir hatten das Prinzip der Laterna magica im Sinn, natürlich auf technisch
anspruchsvollem Niveau, um so etwas wie einen Tagesablauf anzudeuten.

Keller / Veränderung war auch für uns ein Stichwort. Bei den meisten Messe-
ständen habe ich das Gefühl der Wiederkehr des Immergleichen. Selbst die
schönsten Effekte nutzen sich ab. Deshalb hieß unsere Devise: keine Wiederholungen, bitte. Sonst wird der Gedanke der persönlichen Ansprache ad
absurdum geführt: Wenn ich jetzt aufstünde und Ihnen nochmals die Hand
gäbe, würden Sie ja auch denken, was ist mit dem Keller los.

Ingenhoven / Wir wollten, dass die Projektionen eine Art Tagesablauf entwickeln.

Keller / Ein Kontinuum, damit keiner das Gefühl hatte, alles bereits gesehen zu
haben, wenn er zum zweiten Mal kam. Und es ging auch darum, Assoziationen
hervorzurufen, die auf die ausgestellten Fahrzeuge Bezug haben und zugleich
einen emotionalen Zusammenhang zur Haltung des Unternehmens herstellen,
ohne dieses oder jenes Modell explizit zu bewerben.

The design concept not only included the 'loop' as a flowing and transparent large form but also the idea of staging extensive plays of light on its surface. How were the projections on the approximately 2,000 square meters of curved glass set up?

Ingenhoven / We started from the consideration that visitors normally spend hours, sometimes even days at a trade show. They don't see any daylight. It's a dreadful inner world, a black box. We wanted to counter this monotony with a structure, a rhythm: to show moving clouds, a starry sky, underwater images, wheat fields—nature in motion, in other words. We had in mind the principle of the Laterna Magica—at a technologically demanding level, of course—in order to intimate something like the course of a day.

Keller / Change was also a keyword for us. Most exhibition stands give me the feeling of an eternal return of the same. Even the most beautiful effects wear out. That is why our motto was: no repetitions, please. Otherwise, the idea of a personal welcome is reduced to absurdity: if I stood up now and shook your hand again, you would also wonder, what is the matter with this Keller guy.

Ingenhoven / We wanted the projections to imitate the progression of a day.

Keller / A continuum such that no one would have the feeling of already having seen everything if he came by a second time. And we also wanted to evoke associations that relate to the exhibited vehicles and at the same time create an emotional connection to the attitude of the company, without explicitly pro-moting this or that model.

Sie sprachen von ausgefeilter Technik …

Keller / Technisch haben sich die Projektionen als nicht ganz einfaches Problem entpuppt. Schließlich mussten ja horizontal und vertikal gekrümmte Glasflächen so beleuchtet werden, dass szenisch bewegte Bilder mit wechselnden Farbstimmungen darauf entstanden. Und außerdem mussten auf der Glasfläche so hohe Leuchtdichten erzeugt werden, dass sie nicht neben der Fahrzeugpräsentation untergingen.

Die Autos werden also regelrecht mit einem Heiligenschein versehen?

Keller / Es gibt die Tradition bei Audi, auf jedes Auto in Taillenhöhe 5000 Lux Lichtstärke zu setzen, um die Form perfekt zu präsentieren und jedes Fahrzeug zu einer Skulptur zu machen. Diese Bedingung haben wir auf der IAA akzeptiert, und so war es schwierig, andere Lichtakzente zu setzen. Als ich den Verantwortlichen von Audi erstmals die Projektionsidee erläuterte, haben sie mich für völlig verrückt erklärt. Das ist gelegentlich die beste Ausgangssituation, um Dinge mit anderen Augen zu sehen – auch um zum Beispiel dem Wort »visionär« einen konkreten Sinn zu geben.

Sie haben einen ganzen Stab von Experten unter Vertrag genommen, um die Welt des ›Loop‹ in Licht und Bilder zu tauchen.

Ingenhoven / Wir haben Lichttechniker und Spezialisten dabeigehabt, die sonst für große Acts wie Konzerte der Rolling Stones engagiert werden. Die Firma »Four to one« zum Beispiel, zu deren ›Markenzeichen‹ es gehört, die gesamte Beleuchtung und die Projektion im Maßstab 1 : 4 am Modell zu simulieren.

You spoke of sophisticated technology …

Keller / Technically, the projections turned out to pose quite a difficult problem. After all, horizontally and vertically curved glass surfaces had to illuminated in such a way that scenically moving images with changing atmospheres of color would arise on them. And moreover, the luminances generated on the glass surface had to be high enough that they would not be drowned out alongside the presentation of the vehicles.

The cars are thus really decorated with a halo?

Keller / There is the tradition at Audi to create an illuminance of 5000 lux on every car at waist-level, in order to present its form perfectly and to make every vehicle into a sculpture. At the International Auto Show, we accepted this condition, and thus it was difficult to set different lighting accents. When I explained the projection idea for the first time to the people responsible at Audi, they thought I was completely insane. This can sometimes be the best starting point to begin to see things with different eyes—and it also gives the word "visionary" a concrete sense.

You signed on an entire team of experts in order to bathe the world of the 'loop' in light and images.

Ingenhoven / We had lighting technicians and specialists on board, who are otherwise hired for big acts such as concerts of the Rolling Stones. The firm "Four to one", for example, whose 'trademark' it is to simulate, by means of a model, the entire illumination and projection at a scale of 1:4.

Keller / Beim Thema Licht wird der Regie-Aspekt besonders deutlich. Wir haben als künstlerische Leiter eine klare Vision vom Endergebnis, aber weder Architekten noch Designer haben die technischen Kenntnisse, um die Effekte zu realisieren, die sie sich vorgestellt haben. Ein Beispiel: Damit die Projektionen auf der gekrümmten Glasfläche nicht völlig verzerrt erscheinen, mussten sowohl die Linsen der Beamer speziell geschliffen als auch die Bilder im Rechner im Voraus verzerrt werden.

Ingenhoven / Die Beamer mussten so angebracht werden, dass ihr Licht nicht durch die zwei Millimeter breiten Schlitze zwischen den Glasplatten als Raster auf die Autos fallen konnte.

Keller / An die vierzig Beamer waren schließlich im Einsatz und wurden über eine eigens entwickelte Software reguliert.

Ingenhoven / Außerdem hatte der ›Loop‹ am unteren Rand ein durchgängiges Lichtband, für das über hundert Hintergrundleuchten mit eigenem Farbmischsystem installiert wurden. Die wurden ebenfalls über ein Programm, das sich an der Grundfarbe der jeweiligen Bilder orientierte, gesteuert und gedimmt.

Keller / Im Anhang kann man ja nachlesen, wie viele Spezialisten und Firmen in das Projekt involviert waren. Die Ähnlichkeit zum Abspann beim Film ist kein Zufall. Gestalten heißt Regie führen – ob als Architekt oder als Designer. Dazu gehört, die richtigen Partner für jede Aufgabe zu finden und sie zu koordinieren. Oder auch mal zu helfen, vierzig Beamer in der benötigten Leistungsstärke aufzutreiben. Auch das war keineswegs einfach.

Keller / With regard to light, the 'directing' aspect of our work becomes especially clear. As artistic directors, we have a clear vision of the final result, but
neither architects nor designers have the technical know-how to realize the
effects they have in mind. One example: so that the projections on the curved
glass surface do not appear completely distorted, it was necessary both to
grind the lenses of the projectors in a special way and to distort the images in
the computer in advance.

Ingenhoven / The projectors had to be attached in such a way as to prevent
their light from passing through the two millimeters wide slits between the glass
panes and form a grid on the cars.

Keller / Nearly forty projectors were eventually used, which were controlled by
means of specially developed software.

Ingenhoven / In addition, the 'loop' featured a continuous strip of light along
its lower edge, for which more than a hundred background lights with their own
color mixing system were installed. These were likewise controlled and dimmed
by means of a program that responded to the primary color of the respective
images.

Keller / In the appendix, you can look up how many specialists and firms were
involved in the project. The similarity to the final credits of a film is no accident.
Designing means directing—whether you do it as architect or as designer. Part
of this job is to find the right partners for every task and to coordinate them.
Or, on occasion, to help find forty projectors with the required output. This was
by no means easy.

Die Projektionen brauchten eine aufnahmefähige Oberfläche. Je matter jedoch das Glas, desto stärker beeinträchtigt dies die Leichtigkeit der architektonischen Konstruktion. Schließlich haben Sie sich für den Satinierungsgrad 1/1 entschieden. Kann das als Chiffre für die tastende Annäherung von Architektur und Kommunikationsdesign stehen?

Keller / Die Auswahl der geeigneten Glasoberfläche hat uns in der Tat lange beschäftigt. Wie stark dürfen die Scheiben geätzt sein, damit das Glas noch ausreichend transluzent ist und der Architektur gerecht wird? Und welches Glas hat gleichzeitig gute Diffusionseigenschaften, wie wir sie für die Projektion brauchen? Welche Seite des Glases muss dazu geätzt werden? Sieht das Glas dann noch nach Glas aus oder eher nach Plastik, nach etwas Billigem?

Ingenhoven / Besonders schön an dieser konkreten Geschichte ist die Tatsache, dass wir als Zuständige für das Material durch KMS auf den einzigen Lieferanten gestoßen sind, der diese Sonderstufe – 1/1 – der Satinierung produziert. Damit wird der symbolische Gehalt des Kürzels erweitert: Es geht nicht nur um die teilweise schwierige Annäherung, sondern eben auch um praktische Ergänzung.

The projections required a receptive surface. The more frosted the glass, how-ever, the more this will detract from the lightness of the architectural structure. In the end, you decided on a satin-frosting grade of 1/1. Can this be regarded as a code for the tentative rapprochement between architecture and communi-cations design?

Keller / The choice of a suitable glass surface indeed occupied us for a long time. To what degree can the panes be etched such that the glass is still suffi-ciently translucent to do justice to the architecture? And which type of glass has at the same time good diffusive characteristics such as are needed for the projection? Which side of the glass must be etched for this purpose? Will the glass then still look like glass or rather like plastic, like something cheap?

Ingenhoven / A particularly wonderful aspect of this concrete story is the fact that, as people responsible for material, we were able to find, through KMS, the only supplier who produces this special grade—1/1—of satin-frosting. This enriches the symbolic content of the abbreviation: it indicates not merely the sometimes difficult rapprochement, but also a mutual practical completion.

Sie arbeiten mit Bildern, mit Licht und mit Musik. Wie halten Sie die Balance, damit das Spektakel nicht zur Bedröhnung wird?

Ingenhoven / Die Atmosphäre war insgesamt eher sanft und zurückhaltend. Die Musik war leise, mitunter sphärisch, eine Art Klanggewebe. Bei den Projektionen selbst handelte es sich nicht um Filme mit hektischer Bewegung. Die Bilder bestanden eher aus Strukturen, ohne knallige Farbtöne. Es gab also keine Addition von grellen Attraktionen.

Keller / Darin stimmten unsere Konzepte von Anfang an überein. Wir haben unseren Ansatz »Ein Glas Wasser« genannt. Ein Glas Wasser zu reichen, heißt: »Willkommen. Wir kümmern uns um Sie.« Das versteht man auf der ganzen Welt. Und ein Glas Wasser ist ein sehr reales Bedürfnis fast jedes Messebesuchers. Daran denkt man zu wenig. Als Kommunikationsdesigner verstehen wir es als wesentlichen Teil unserer Aufgabe, dafür zu sorgen, dass es da ist. Das Glas Wasser ist so gesehen ein Symbol für all die Dinge, die mit dem Sich-Wohlfühlen zu tun haben.

Zum Beispiel?

Keller / Dass die Musik in jeder Bucht unterschiedlich war und an den Übergängen trotzdem keine Kakophonien ergab. Dass Bilder und Töne im Random-Verfahren wechselten und dadurch keine stereotype Wiederholung entstand. Dass jeder Besucher fand, was er suchte, ohne in einer Informationsflut unterzugehen. Dass es eine Kinderbetreuung gab. Und dass man sich tatsächlich ein Glas Wasser nehmen konnte.

You work with images, with light and with music. How do you maintain a balance so that the spectacle does not become numbing to the senses?

Ingenhoven / The atmosphere on the whole was rather peaceful and reserved. The music was quiet, at times like music of the spheres, a kind of texture of sounds. The projection itself did not involve films with hectic movement. The images consisted rather of structures without loud tones of color. In other words, there was no addition of shrill attractions.

Keller / Our plans agreed on this point from the beginning. We called our approach "a glass of water". To offer a glass of water means: "Welcome. We will look after you." This is understood the world over. And a glass of water is a very real need for almost every trade show visitor. This is usually given too little consideration. As communications designers, we regard it as an essential part of our task to ensure that it is there. From this perspective, the glass of water is a symbol for all the things connected to one's sense of well-being.

For example?

Keller / That the music was different in every bay, and that nevertheless no cacophonies resulted in between. That images and sounds changed randomly so as to avoid stereotypical repetition. That every visitor found what he was looking for without drowning in a flood of information. That there was child care. And that one was indeed able to take a glass of water.

Ingenhoven / Man darf aber auch nicht vergessen, dass es an den Pressetagen, an denen der Andrang nicht so groß ist, noch möglich sein mag, eine zurück- haltende Atmosphäre zu vermitteln. An den Publikumstagen allerdings bewegt man sich durch Wände von Menschen. Dann ist es zwar noch möglich, das Image einer überwältigenden Form zu transportieren. Die Chancen allerdings, zum Wohlbefinden der 5000 oder 6000 Besucher pro Stunde beizutragen, wenn sich die Halle obendrein durch die Scheinwerfer-Batterien aufgeheizt hat, schätze ich eher als gering ein.

Keller / Entscheidend ist die grundsätzliche Haltung. Man kann keine Wunder vollbringen, aber eine Geste zeigen. Das Wie ist wichtiger als das Was. Nach unserer Auffassung von Messe-Design besteht kein grundsätzlicher Unterschied zwischen gestalterischen und Gastgeber-Aufgaben. Was nützt eine subtile Farbauswahl für die Besucher-Lounge, wenn diese zu klein ist oder zu laut und niemand sich dort ausruhen kann?

Eine Art Wellness-Projekt?

Ingenhoven / Lassen Sie mich einmal so fragen: Was nimmt jemand von so einem Messetag mit? Berauschende Architektur, schnelle Autos? Oder erst einmal ganz einfach, dass er sich wohl gefühlt hat? Das sollte man keinesfalls gering schätzen. Natürlich bekommt er auch das Sicherheitssystem der Autos erklärt, mit Filmen und mit Modellen für Millionen von Mark. Kommunikations- angebote gibt es zuhauf, selbst in der Farbwahl der ausgestellten Autos steckt eines. In den gedruckten Informationen. In der Gestaltung der Broschüren und der Visitenkarten, in den Give-aways, ja in der Frage, wie das Essen schmeckt. Das Messegeschehen ist heute angefüllt mit völlig unterschiedlichen Ebenen der Kommunikation. Und die Architektur ist eine davon.

Ingenhoven / It may indeed still be possible to convey a reserved atmosphere on days when the show is only open to the press and there is not such a great crush. On days that are open to the public, however, one moves through walls of people. To be sure, it is then still possible to convey the image of an overwhelming form. The chances, however, of contributing to the well-being of the 5,000 or 6,000 visitors per hour, when the hall, to top it all, has been heated up by the batteries of floodlights, I regard as rather low.

Keller / What is crucial is the fundamental attitude. One cannot perform miracles, but one can make a gesture. The 'how' is more important than the 'what'. In our conception of trade show design there is no fundamental difference between designing tasks and hosting tasks. What good is a subtle choice of colors for the visitors lounge, when the lounge is too small or too noisy and does not offer rest to anyone.

A type of wellness project?

Ingenhoven / Let me ask the following: what does a visitor take away from such a day at a trade show? Breathtaking architecture, fast cars? Or, first of all, simply the fact that he felt comfortable. This should in no way be underestimated. Of course, the safety system of the cars is also explained to him, with films and with models worth millions of Marks. There are numerous communications offerings. There is even one in the choice of color of the displayed cars. In printed information booklets. In the design of brochures and business cards, in the giveaways, even in the question of the taste of the food. Today, events at trade shows are filled with completely different levels of communication. And architecture is one them.

Audi fertigt sehr unterschiedliche Modelle. Wie haben Sie im ›Loop‹ die einzelnen Buchten, sozusagen die Subwelten, eingerichtet, damit sie die passende Umgebung für die jeweiligen Produktfamilien abgeben?

Ingenhoven / Ich glaube nicht, dass die Typen so unterschiedlich sind. Natürlich versucht jeder Autohersteller, mit seiner Produktpalette das gesamte Spektrum vom Single bis zur Großfamilie, von Jung bis Alt abzudecken. Das bedeutet aber nicht, dass sich die Identität der Marke nicht auf alle Typen übertragen ließe. Mit dem ›Loop‹ haben wir eine flexible Form gebaut. Die Halbnischen, in denen die verschiedenen Fahrzeugfamilien Platz finden, unterscheiden sich architektonisch nicht.

Keller / Für uns sah das etwas anders aus. Für jedes Fahrzeug gibt es eine eigene Marketingstrategie. Wir bekommen ein Hundert-Seiten-Papier über Positionierung, Zielgruppen und technische Details. Ein A4 hat nun einmal eine komplett andere Zielgruppe als der A8 meinetwegen. Im ›Loop‹ konnten wir die Produktgruppen gut voneinander trennen und unterschiedlich positionieren. Außerdem hatten wir ein Konzept entwickelt, das auf aktives Sammeln von Einzelinformationen setzte statt auf Überschüttung. Jeder Besucher bekam ein leeres Portfolio, in welchem er technische Daten über die Modelle, die ihn interessierten, individuell zusammenstellen konnte.

Audi produces very different models. How did you set up the individual bays inside the 'loop'—the sub-worlds, so to speak—so that they make suitable environments for the respective product families?

Ingenhoven / I don't think that the models are all that different. Every automaker, of course, attempts to cover the entire spectrum of consumers with its product line, from single people to large families, from the young up to the elderly. But this does not mean that the identity of the make cannot be transferred to all models. With the 'loop', we have built a flexible form. The semi-recesses, in which the various families of vehicles are housed, are not differentiated architecturally.

Keller / We saw this a bit differently from our perspective. For every vehicle there is a particular marketing strategy. We received a one hundred page document regarding positioning, target groups and technical details. An A4, after all, has a completely different target group than an A8, for example. The 'loop' allowed for a neat separation of the product groups and for variation in their positioning. In addition, we had developed a concept where visitors would actively collect individual items of information rather than being swamped with information, as is commonly done. Every visitor received an empty portfolio, in which he could assemble a customized set of technical data about models that interested him.

Das ist relativ ungewöhnlich …

Keller / Ja, so ungewöhnlich, dass letztlich doch sehr viele Fahrzeuginformationen als Basis-Satz vorab in das Portfolio gewandert sind. Wenn es konkret um die Autos geht, sind Experimente bei Automobilkonzernen nicht sehr erwünscht.

Ingenhoven / Ähnlich war es bei der Fahrzeugpräsentation. Nicht nur in Bezug auf die Beleuchtung, sondern auch bei der Wahl der Farben und bei der Aufstellung konnten wir so gut wie gar nicht mitreden. Und so wurden die Autos relativ hilflos hingestellt, ohne eigene Dynamik, wie beim Händler. Ich denke, die Wagen müssten wie ein Rudel wirken, das auf einen zukommt. Eine Rotte müsste man hinbekommen. Oder es müsste so wie eine Startaufstellung für ein Rennen aussehen, eine etwas nervöse, spannungsreiche Konstellation.

Dafür gab es zusätzliche Installationen wie den so genannten Monitorwald, die nicht gerade die Wirkung des ›Loop‹ unterstützen …

Keller / Wir haben den Monitorwald für die Präsentation des A2 entwickelt, der auf der IAA Weltpremiere hatte. Christoph Ingenhoven befürchtete tatsächlich, wir würden ihm den ganzen ›Loop‹ damit verbauen. Doch wir mussten uns etwas einfallen lassen, um das Highlight zu inszenieren. Durch die Installation aus vielen kleinen Bildschirmen, die immer wieder ein virtuelles Gesamtbild zeigen, konnten wir es vermeiden, eine zweite Wand aufzubauen, die dann den ›Loop‹ tatsächlich verdeckt hätte. Andererseits ist der Monitorwald auch unabhängig vom Gesamtkontext von vielen positiv aufgenommen worden.

This is quite unusual …

Keller / Yes, it is so unusual that, in the end, a basic set of information about the vehicles nevertheless found its way into the portfolio in advance. When it concerns the cars themselves, automakers are not very fond of experiments.

Ingenhoven / It was a similar situation in the case of the presentation of the vehicles. Not only with respect to lighting, but also in the choice of colors and in the set-up, we virtually had no say at all. And thus the cars were placed looking quite awkward and without any inner dynamism, as in a car dealership. I think the cars should appear like a pack of wolves approaching the viewer. It should be possible to create this mob-like impression. Or you create the appearance of a set-up for a race, a somewhat nervous, charged constellation.

Instead there were additional installations such as the so-called monitor forest, which do not exactly enhance the effect of the 'loop'…

Keller / We created the monitor forest for the presentation of the A2, which had its world premiere at the International Auto Show. Christoph Ingenhoven indeed feared that we would spoil his entire 'loop' with it. Yet, we had to come up with something to stage the highlight of the show. Through the installation of many small monitors, which together always present a new virtual picture, we were able to avoid constructing a second wall that would indeed have blocked the view of the 'loop'. On the other hand, the monitor forest got a positive reception by many, even independently of the overall context.

Ingenhoven / Man mochte offenbar nicht einer Kommunikationsebene allein vertrauen. Dabei gäbe es meiner Meinung nach Strategien, die ausschließlich mit Architektur arbeiten. Architektur hat ein hohes Prestige und eine hohe kulturelle Avantgardefähigkeit. Man hätte ihr mehr vertrauen sollen. Man hätte zusätzliche Informationen addieren können, sie aber nicht als vorrangig behandeln sollen. Die Hersteller dürfen nicht dem Impuls folgen, immer noch mehr Autos, noch mehr Farben, schließlich den gesamten Katalog ausstellen zu wollen. Das führt zu einer Verflachung. Ich träume nach wie vor von einem Messeauftritt mit nur fünf Autos auf 5000 Quadratmetern, alle fünf silberfarben.

Keller / Wir haben mehrere Jahre an einem Konzept für ein BMW-Museum gearbeitet und planten es sogar ganz ohne Autos. Jetzt haben wir das Museum für Audi gestaltet – mit Fahrzeugen, wohlgemerkt. Es kommt immer auf die Schlüssigkeit der Idee an, man kann das nicht grundsätzlich festlegen.

Ingenhoven / Die Botschaft, man wolle die Emotionalität einer Marke fortentwickeln, kann man nur radikal formulieren. Wenn man anfängt, sie politisch korrekt zu machen, damit jeder sein Häppchen bekommt, entsteht der Eindruck eines Gemischtwarenladens. Die Aussagen müssen klar und deutlich sein, sonst verflüchtigen sie sich angesichts der ständig wachsenden Informationsflut. Man kann nicht vierzig Autos aufstellen und die Besucher auch noch mit Details überschütten.

Ingenhoven / The client obviously didn't want to rely exclusively on one level of communication. But in my opinion there are strategies that could have worked exclusively with architecture. Architecture enjoys a high prestige and the ability to assume the role of a cultural avant-garde. One should have placed more faith in it. Additional information could have been supplied without giving it priority treatment. Manufacturers must not act on the impulse to want to exhibit more and more cars, even more colors and finally the entire catalogue. This leads to superficiality. I still dream of an exhibition with only five cars on 5,000 square meters, all five of them in silver.

Keller / For several years, we worked on a plan for a BMW museum and even conceived it completely without cars. Now we designed the museum for Audi —with vehicles, mind you. It all depends on how convincing your idea is. This has to be determined from case to case.

Ingenhoven / The message of wanting to develop the emotionality of a make can only be formulated in a radical way. If you begin to render it politically correct so as to offer a special tidbit to everyone, you give the impression of a general store. The statements have to be clear and distinct. Otherwise they will evaporate in the face of the constantly growing flood of information. You cannot set up forty cars and on top of it swamp visitors with details.

Keller / Apropos Radikalität: Für Lamborghini haben wir auf der Messe 1998 in Paris ein Bassin aufgestellt, das bis zum Rand mit Flüssigkeit angefüllt war – ein scharfkantiger, schwarzer Block, über dem die Fahrzeuge in Kopfhöhe der Besucher schwebend installiert waren. »Ins Auge schauen« lautete das Thema. Der Eindruck einer festen Oberfläche führte dazu, dass viele Gegenstände darauf ›abgestellt‹ wurden und im Bassin verschwanden, darunter eine Fernsehkamera. Die Lamborghini-Verantwortlichen wurden nervös und kapitulierten beim sechsunddreißigsten Zwischenfall. Ist das der Lamborghini-Wert? 36? Ich meine, dass der Betrag, den sie für die ruinierten Objekte zahlen mussten, lächerlich gegenüber dem ist, was dieser Auftritt an Kraft auf die Messe brachte. Lamborghini ist eben eine radikale Marke.

Nicht jede Ihrer Installationen für Audi hat mit Radikalität zu tun. Welche Idee steckt zum Beispiel hinter dem Motorenscanner?

Keller / Motorenbau gehört nun einmal zu den Kernkompetenzen von Audi. Also sollen Motoren auch gezeigt werden. Wir wollten sie aber nicht einfach nur als eine Art Ikone aufstellen, wie es bislang der Fall war. Darum kam uns die Idee mit dem Scanner, der den Motor gleichsam durchleuchtet. Per Touchscreen kann der Besucher den hin- und herfahrenden Scanner an jeder Stelle anhalten und sich anhand einer Animation einzelne Details erklären lassen – der Motor spricht gewissermaßen mit ihm.

Keller / Talking about radical: at the show in Paris in 1998, we set up a tank for Lamborghini that was filled to the brim with a liquid—a sharp-edged, black block, above which die vehicles were installed, hovering at eye-level. The theme was "straight into the eyes". The impression of a solid surface lead to the result that many objects, which were 'placed' on this surface, disappeared in the tank, among them a television camera. The people responsible at Lamborghini became nervous and capitulated at the thirty-sixth incident. Is this Lamborghini's value? 36? I mean that the sum that they had to pay for the ruined objects was ridiculous compared to the energy that this appearance brought to the show. Lamborghini is, after all, a radical brand.

Not all of your installations for Audi have this radical aspect. What, for example, is the idea behind the motor scanner?

Keller / Motor construction is, after all, one of Audi's core strengths. Hence, motors should also be displayed. But we did not want to set them up merely as a type of icon, as was done in the past. This is why we came up with the idea of the scanner, which x-rays the motor, as it were. By means of a touch screen, visitors can stop the scanner at any point on the path along which it moves back and forth and can obtain explanations of individual details through an animation. The motor speaks with the visitors, as it were.

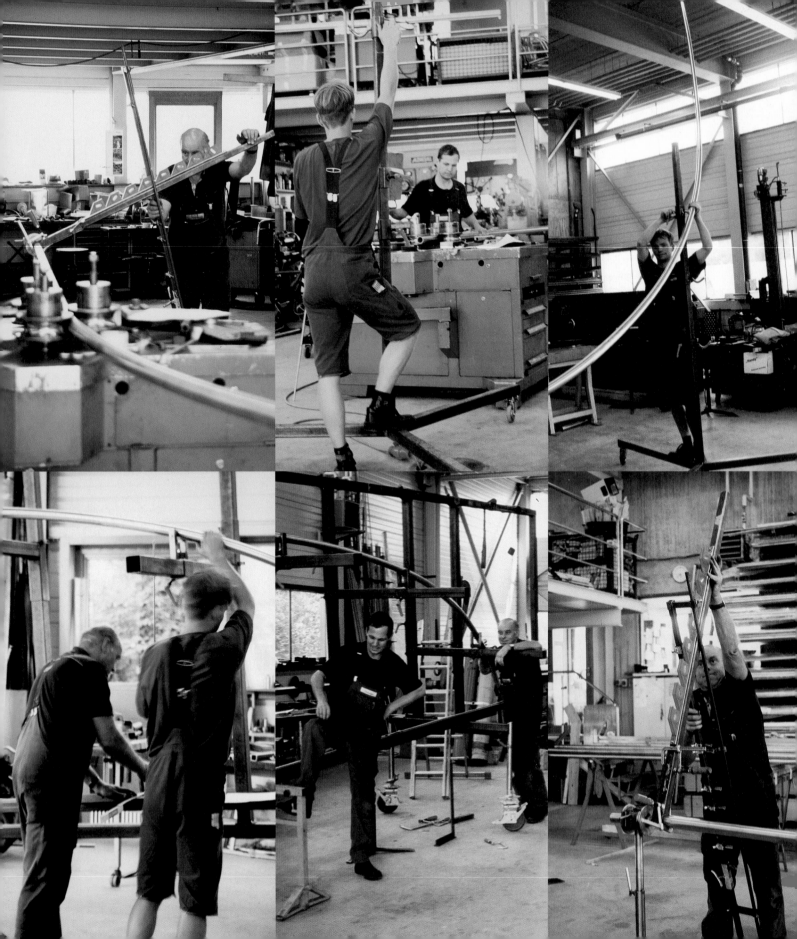

10101

Der Bau des ›Loop‹ hat mehrere Millionen Mark gekostet, der gesamte Auftritt noch einmal so viel. Mehr als ein halbes Jahr haben Sie geplant, für den Aufbau hatten Sie dagegen exakt sieben Tage Zeit.

Ingenhoven / Dass wir nur sieben Tage für den Aufbau haben würden, war von Anfang an klar. Deswegen hätten wir vielleicht total clever vorgehen und ein Messekonzept entwerfen sollen, das dem Rechnung trägt. Haben wir aber nicht, muss ich selbstkritisch sagen. Stattdessen haben wir einen ziemlich verrückten Entwurf abgeliefert, der fast nicht baubar war und für den wir eine Einzelzulassung für die Konstruktion brauchten. Aber die Antwort »Das geht nicht« hören wir ja ohnehin viel zu oft im Leben. Es ist ein Stück konstruktionsbestimmte Architektur dabei herausgekommen, das die übliche Messebau-Logistik fast aus den Angeln hebt. Aber es hat ja funktioniert.

Alles eine Frage der Logistik?

Ingenhoven / Von Anfang an war auch die Firma Ambrosius als Generalunternehmer für Messebau eingeschaltet, die uns schon während des Wettbewerbs beraten hatte. Die haben uns zwar zwischendurch auch mal für wahnsinnig erklärt, aber schließlich haben sie es gebaut. Das war eine Herausforderung für solche Profis, und das hat sie auch gereizt. Manchmal haben 200 Handwerker gleichzeitig auf der Baustelle gearbeitet.

The construction of the 'loop' cost several millions of Marks, and the exhibition as a whole cost several millions more. You were planning for more than half a year. For the set-up, by contrast, you were allotted exactly seven days.

Ingenhoven / It was clear from the beginning that we would only have seven days for the set-up. For this reason, we would perhaps have been wise to design an exhibit that took this time constraint into account. I must concede that we failed to do that. Instead, we submitted a pretty crazy design, which was almost unworkable, and for which we required a special construction permit. But in life, we all too often hear the response, "that's not going to work". Our venture resulted in a piece of structurally defined architecture, which almost turns the usual construction logistics at trade shows upside down. But it worked.

Is it all a question of logistics?

Ingenhoven / From the beginning, the firm Ambrosius, which had already advised us during the competition, was also engaged as general contractor for trade show construction. It is true that from time to time they also thought that we were insane, but they built our design in the end. That was a challenge for such professionals, but it attracted them as well. Sometimes we had 200 trades people working on the construction site.

Keller / Und Tokio stand auch schon vor der Tür …

Ingenhoven / Ja, parallel dazu mussten wir den ›Loop‹ für die Messe in Tokio konstruieren, die nur wenig später begann. Noch vor Beginn des Aufbaus in Frankfurt musste alles nach Japan verschifft worden sein. Das Projekt wäre im Zweifelsfall nicht zu retten gewesen. Wir mussten uns vollständig auf die Professionalität der Firmen verlassen. Aber auch bei uns im Büro war der Aufwand in der Planungsphase außergewöhnlich groß. Es ist etwas anderes, ob man einen Auftrag ganz normal über vier Jahre – ein Jahr Planung, ein Jahr Ausschreibung und Genehmigung und zwei Jahre Bauzeit – abwickelt oder in sechs Monaten. Wir waren als Generalplaner tätig, hatten Tragwerksplaner, Haustechniker, Lichtplaner, alle hatten wir unter Vertrag. Messebau war ein völlig neues Kapitel für uns; wir hatten nicht die geringste Vorstellung, was uns erwartet.

Keller / And Tokyo was also just around the corner …

Ingenhoven / Yes, in parallel, we had to construct the 'loop' for the Tokyo Motor Show, which was to begin just a little later. Even before construction began in Frankfurt, everything had to be shipped to Japan. In case of a mishap, it would have been impossible to save the project. We had to rely completely on the professionalism of the firms involved. But even in our office, the efforts were exceptionally great during the planning phase. It is a different thing, whether one fulfills a contract in the normal way over a span of four years—one year of planning, one year for tendering and approval and two years of construction—or in six months. We acting as general planners and had supporting framework planners, building engineers and lighting designers under contract. Trade show construction was a completely new chapter for us. We didn't have the slightest idea of what we were getting into.

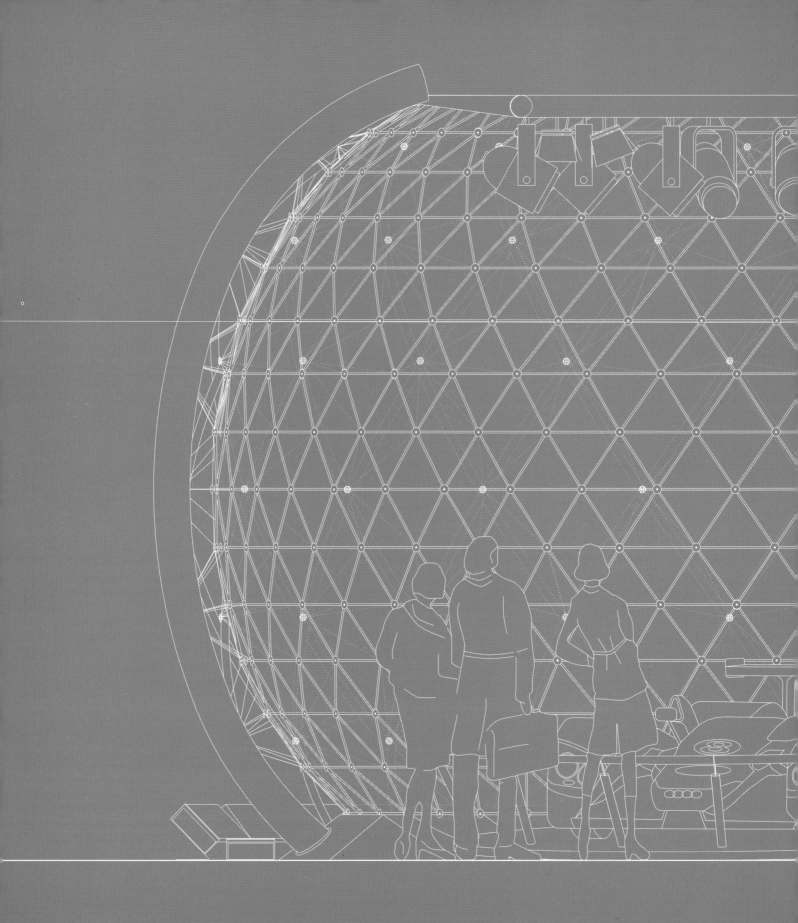

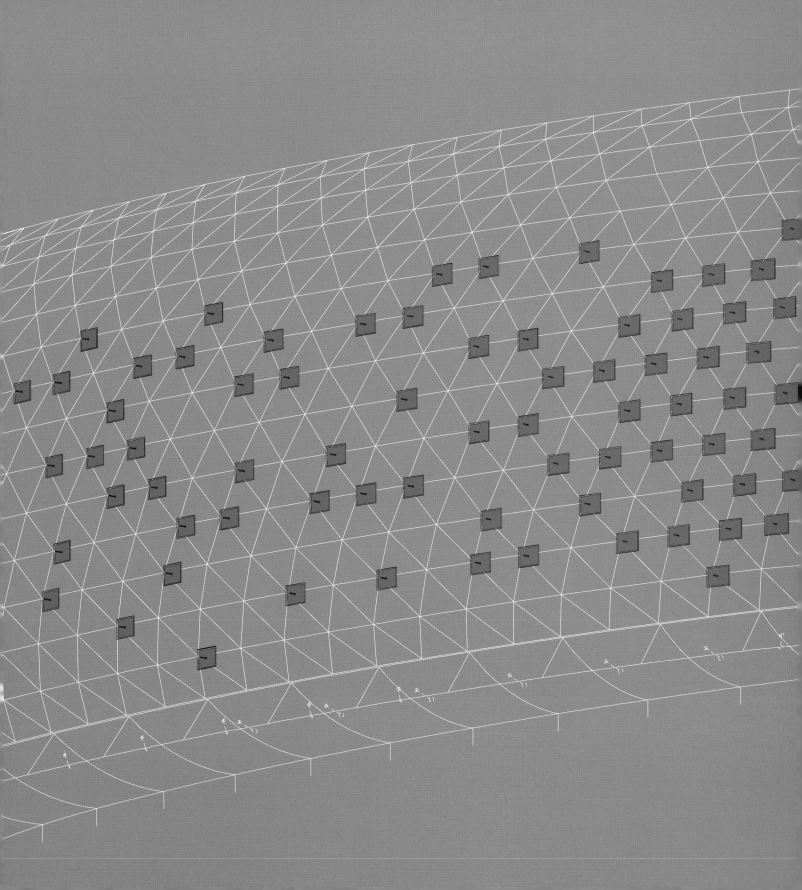

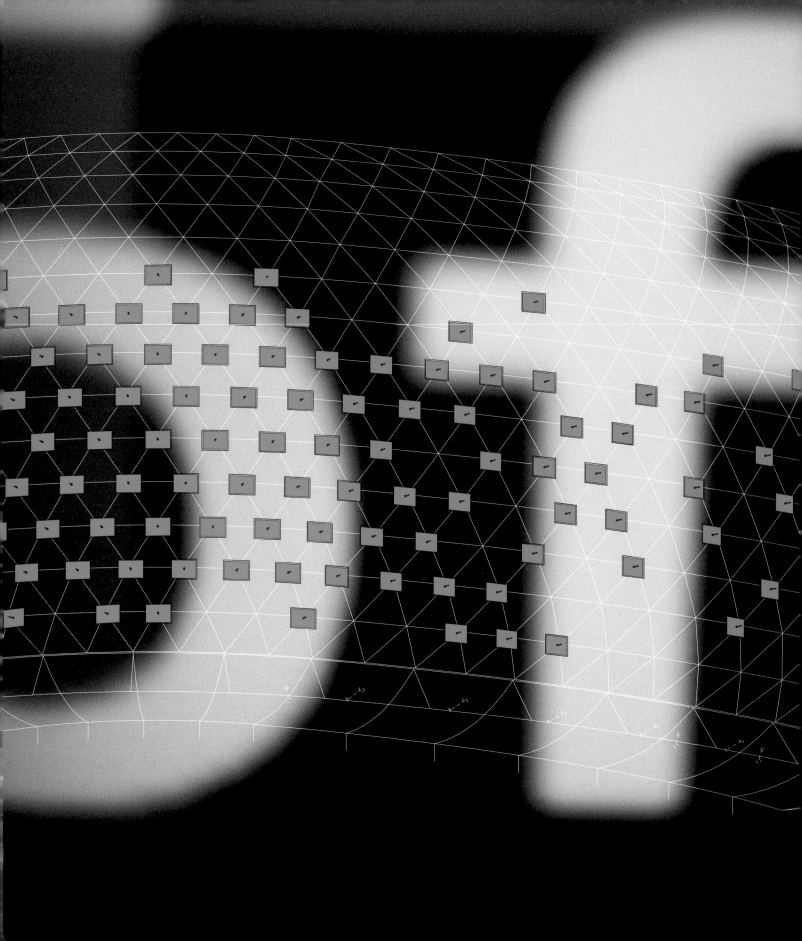

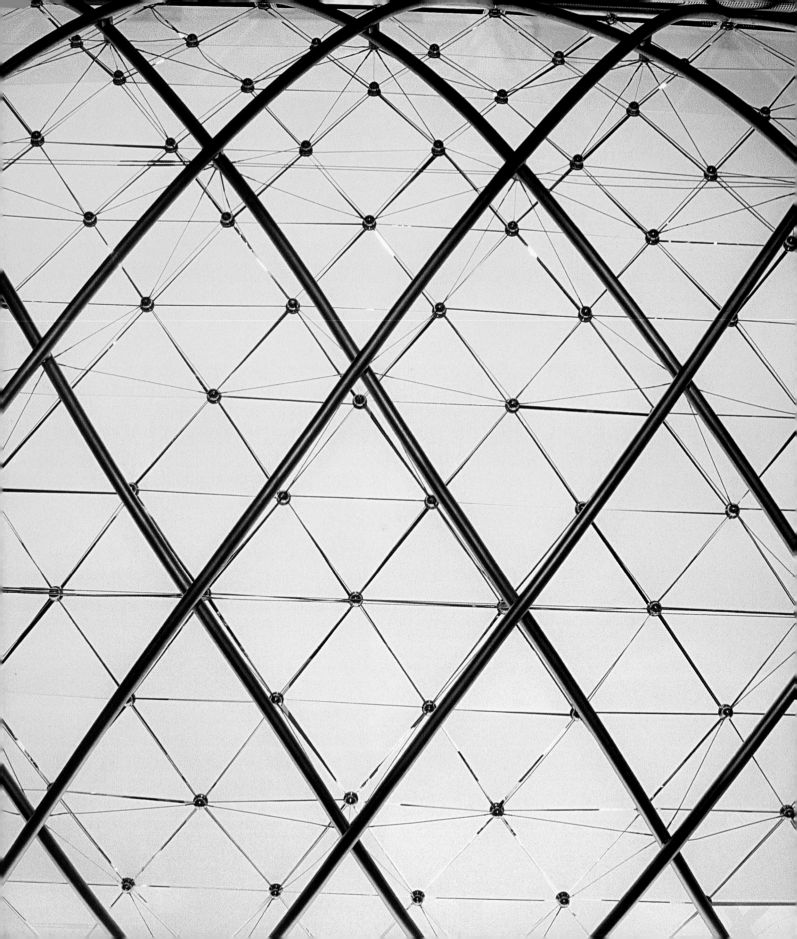

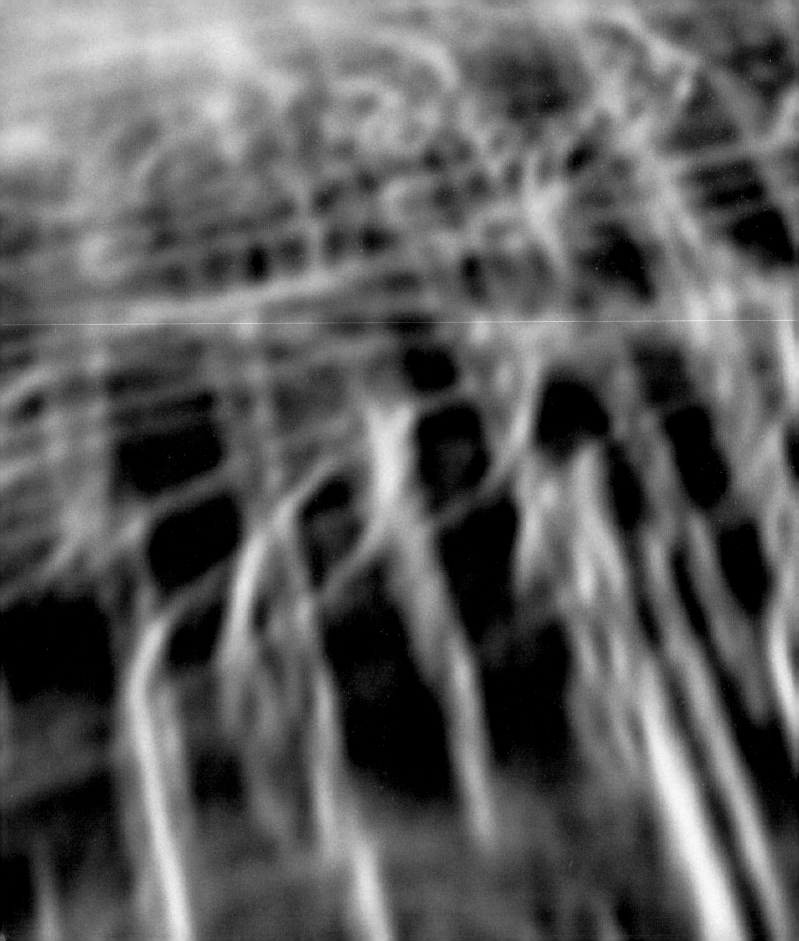

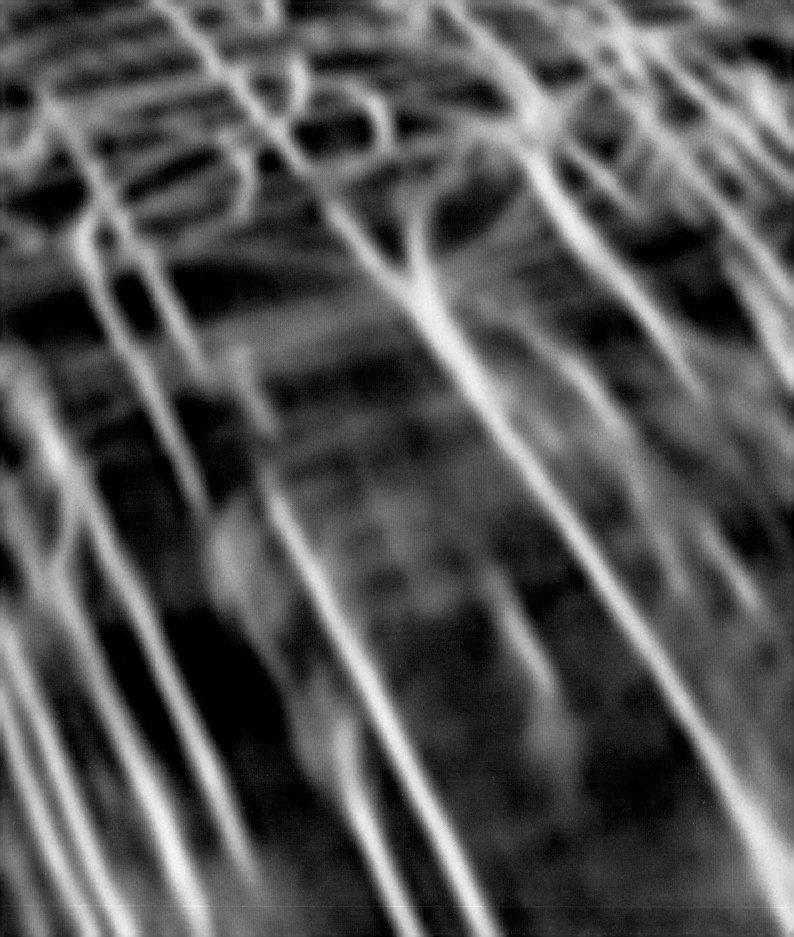

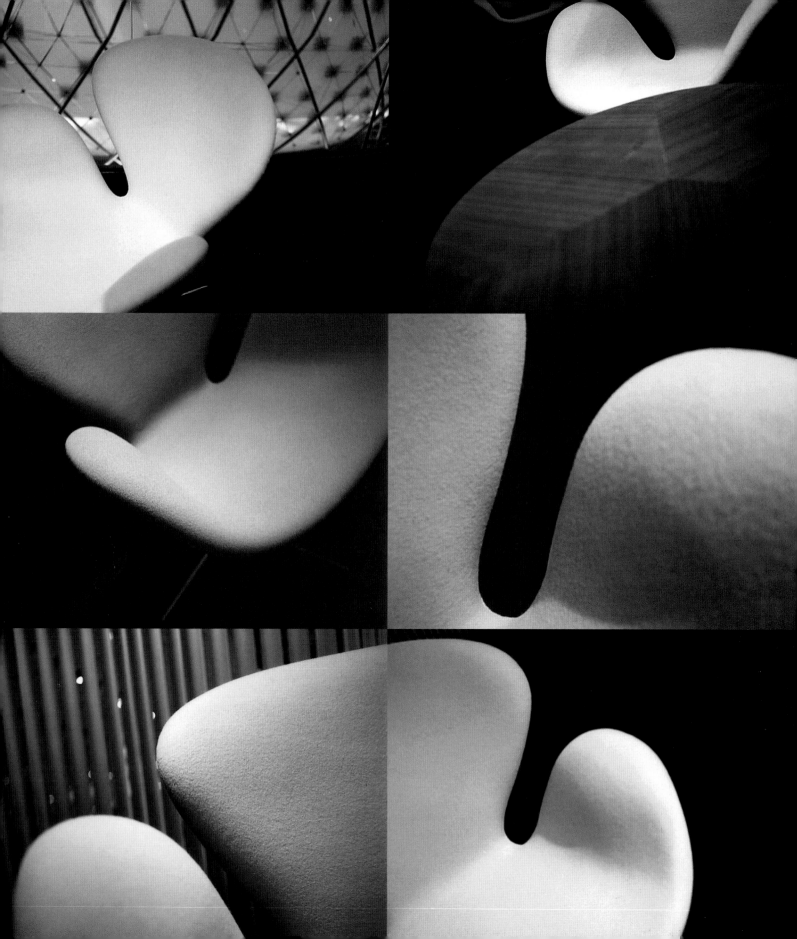

Touchscreen
Bewegen Sie den Monitor an den Punkt Ihres Interesses.
Berühren Sie die Icons auf dem Bildschirm.
So erfahren Sie alles Wissenswerte über den Motor.

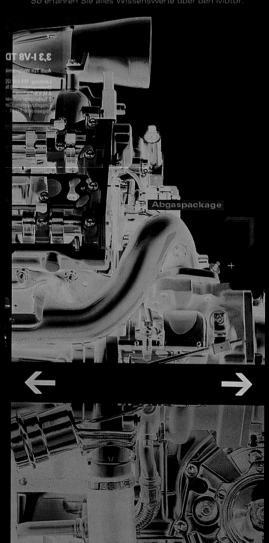

Abgaspackage

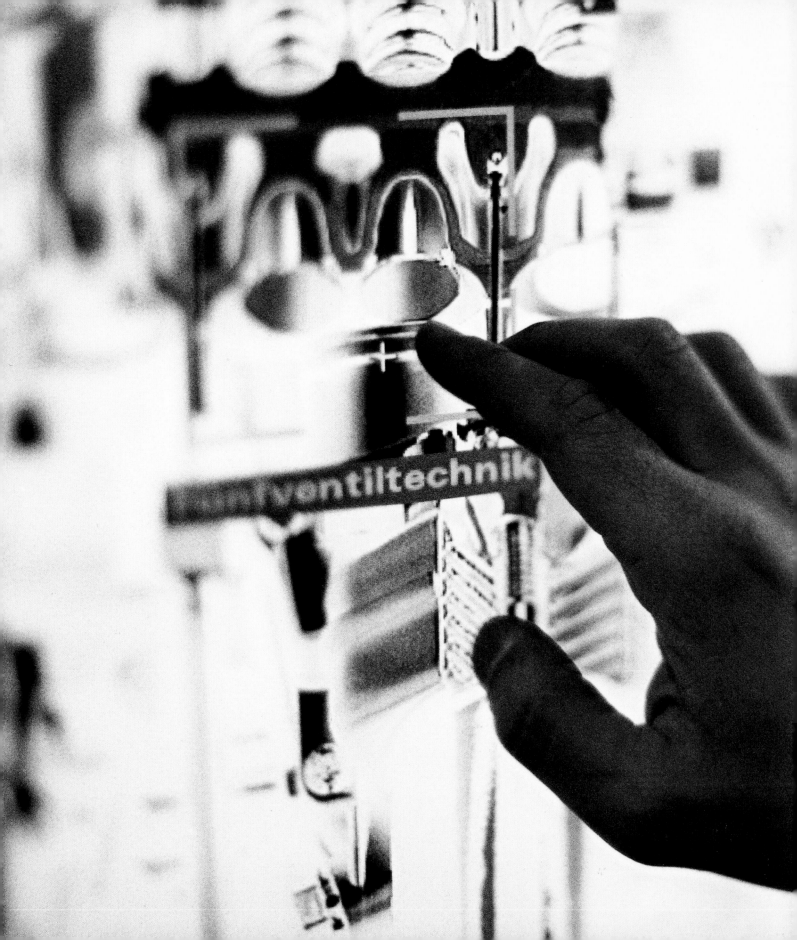

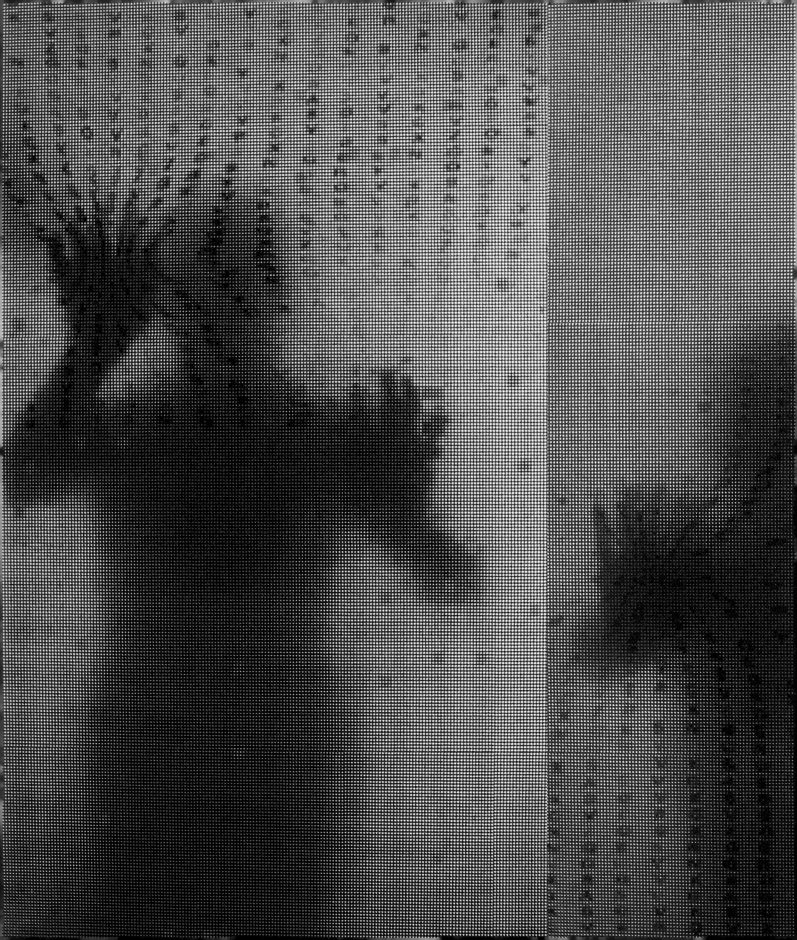

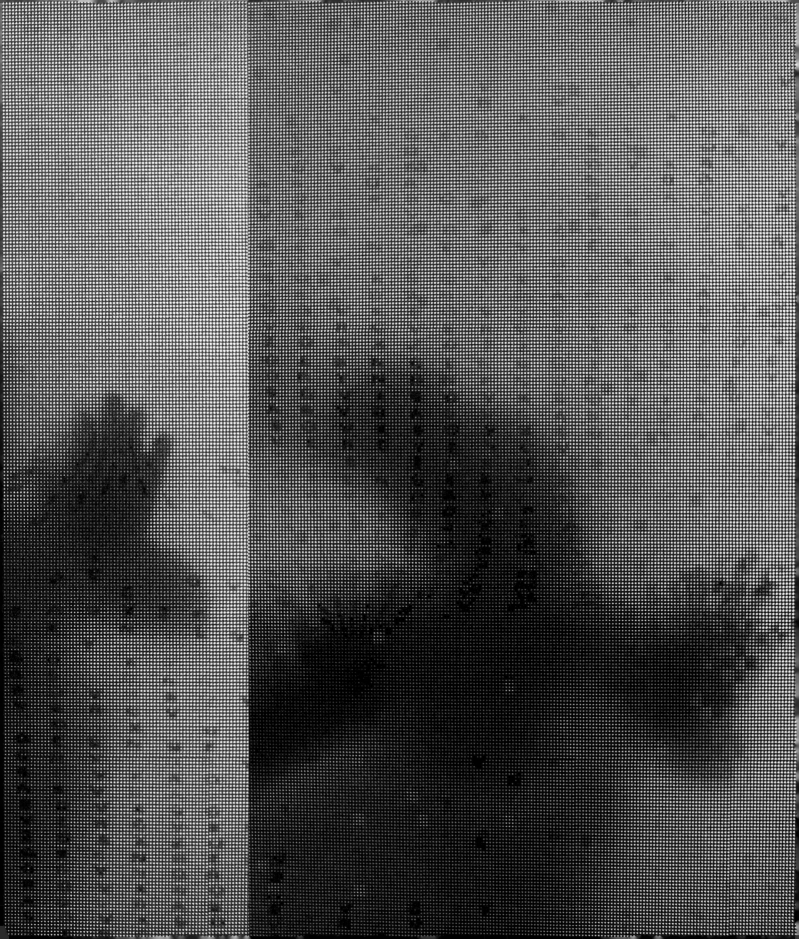

Sie hatten ja schon Erfahrung auf diesem Gebiet.

Keller / Unsere Arbeit lief parallel zu der des Büros Ingenhoven, aber es ist eine völlig andere Art der Planung. Während es in Düsseldorf beispielsweise um die Stahlkonstruktion ging, fragten wir uns, wie sich die einzelnen Highlights inszenieren lassen. Wir sind sehr oft beim Kunden, manchmal drei Tage in der Woche. Bei uns geht es immer wieder auch um das schnelle Reagieren. Die Frage der Architektur wird früh entschieden, danach ist das Thema so gut wie durch. Unser Konzept dagegen wird immer wieder aktualisiert und vom Vorstand begutachtet.

Ingenhoven / Auch wir müssen manchmal um kleine Details sehr lange verhandeln. Audi zum Beispiel wollte Tische aus Kirschbaumholz in den Lounges, die wirklich ganz und gar nicht zum gesamten Auftritt passten. Letztlich haben wir sie dann doch als einen der kleinen Schmerzpunkte akzeptieren müssen, aber die Verantwortlichen waren erstaunt, dass wir Widerworte gaben.

Haben Sie oft diesen Streit um die kleinen Geschmacklosigkeiten, um die kleinen Zumutungen?

Ingenhoven / Wir bekommen meistens den kompletten Auftrag: mit Innenarchitektur, mit Möblierung, mit allem Drum und Dran. Irgendwann kommt bei jedem Projekt der Punkt, an dem der Auftraggeber sein rosafarbenes Sofa will und es irgendwie durchsetzt, sei es, indem er einen Bekannten heranzieht, der Innenarchitekt ist. Das ist wahrscheinlich eine Art Ventil, das notwendig ist.

You already had experience in this area.

Keller / Our work unfolded parallel to that of the Ingenhoven firm, but it is a completely different kind of planning. While in Düsseldorf people were working on the steel structure, we were asking ourselves, how the individual highlights could be staged. We frequently spend time at the client's premises, sometimes three days a week. In our profession, it is often necessary to react quickly. The question of the architecture is decided at an early stage. After that the topic is as good as settled. Our plan, by contrast, is constantly updated and examined by the board of directors.

Ingenhoven / Sometimes, we also spend a long time negotiating small details. Audi, for example, wanted tables made of cherrywood in the lounges, something that really did not fit at all with the exhibit as a whole. In the end, we had to accept them anyway as one of those small painful concessions, but the people responsible were surprised by our backtalk.

Do you often have this quarrel about the small request against good taste, the small impositions?

Ingenhoven / We usually obtain the complete contract: including interior design, furnishings, all the trimmings. With every project, there comes a point at which the client wants his pink sofa and somehow pushes it through, be it by bringing in an acquaintance who is an interior designer. This is probably a kind of release valve, one that is necessary.

Keller / Wir sind in ständigen Abstimmungsgesprächen mit dem Auftraggeber. Natürlich müssen wir auch darauf achten, dass da nicht plötzlich der Standard-Gummibaum aus den Showrooms vor den ›Loop‹ gestellt wird …

Ingenhoven / Schrecklich, ich erinnere mich.

Keller / Aber grundsätzlich ist Kommunikationsdesign für Messen mit einem Formel-1-Rennstall vergleichbar, wo dauernd auf Temperatur, Feuchtigkeit, Windverhältnisse, Luftdruck und was weiß ich alles reagiert werden muss. Es geht um Präzision, und die ist nur mit Konzepten zu erreichen, die flexibel sind.

Warum spielt die Feinabstimmung eine so große Rolle?

Keller / Es gibt verschiedene Faktoren. Einer davon ist, dass unsere Zeichen-sprache in aller Welt funktionieren muss. Setzen wir zum Beispiel die Farbe Weiß ein, müssen wir berücksichtigen, dass sie in Fernost Trauer bedeutet – solcher Details gibt es viele, und man kann sie nicht alle kennen. Also müssen wir stündlich darauf gefasst sein, etwas zu ändern. Ein anderer Punkt sind die marktpolitischen Umstände, die sehr stark schwanken können. Ein Messeauf-tritt muss äußerst sensibel auf die jeweils herrschende Situation reagieren, da kann man nicht alles ein halbes Jahr vorher festlegen. Die Anpassung von Details gehört zum Auftrag.

Keller / We are constantly in coordination meetings with the client. Of course, we must watch out that the standard rubber plant from the showrooms isn't suddenly placed in front of the 'loop'…

Ingenhoven / Horrible, I remember.

Keller / But, fundamentally, communications design for trade shows is comparable to a Formula 1 team, where it is necessary to react constantly to temperature, humidity, wind conditions, air pressure and who knows what else. It is about precision, and this can only be achieved by means of flexible plans.

Why does fine-tuning play such a large role?

Keller / There are various factors. One of them is that our sign language must work around the world. If we use the color white, for example, we must consider that it signifies mourning in the Far East. There are many such details, and one cannot be aware of them all. Hence, we must be prepared to change something from one hour to the next. Another issue is market conditions, which may fluctuate a great deal. A trade show exhibit must react very sensitively to the prevailing conditions. One cannot determine everything half a year in advance. The adjustment of details is part of the contract.

Ingenhoven / Architects loathe these kinds of discussions. But in fact, much of what we do is simply providing a service. The important thing is: one must not confuse it with shining shoes. One should not be able to detect a social difference in the relation between client and architect. Most often, we have a position of equality and do not first have to fight for it. One must only take care not to stagnate in the long tunnel of middle management.

Ingenhoven / Das sind Diskussionen, die Architekten ungern führen. Aber tatsächlich ist vieles von dem, was wir tun, schlicht eine Dienstleistung. Man darf es nur nicht mit Schuhe putzen verwechseln. In dem Verhältnis zwischen Bauherrn und Architekten sollte man keine soziale Differenz erkennen. Meistens haben wir eine gleichberechtigte Position und müssen sie uns auch nicht erst erkämpfen. Man darf nur nicht im langen Tunnel des mittleren Managements versauern.

Müssen Sie sich im Normalfall von den Auftraggebern hineinreden lassen?

Ingenhoven / Nein, das habe ich mein ganzes Berufsleben über nicht erlebt. Das wäre so, als wenn der Auftraggeber eines Künstlers meinte, da er eine Million für das Bild bezahlt habe, dürfe er auch entscheiden, welche Farbe es hat. Das ist ein kulturelles Missverständnis. Wir halten es für völlig normal zu widersprechen. Ich meine, dass der Architekt nicht sein Honorar dafür bekommt, dass er ständig »Ja« sagt, sondern dafür, dass er »Nein« sagt. Sonst könnte der Bauherr sich einfach ein paar Bauzeichner holen. Ein anderes Beispiel: Man engagiert nicht einen sündteuren Rechtsanwalt für 1000 Mark die Stunde und erklärt ihm dann noch die Prozessstrategie. Da muss man schon ein bisschen Vertrauen haben.

Keller / Architekten haben in dieser Hinsicht eine bessere Ausgangsposition. Als Kommunikationsdesigner muss ich wesentlich mehr Überzeugungsarbeit leisten.

Is it not normally the case that clients meddle in your work?

Ingenhoven / No, I have not experienced that in my entire professional life. That would be like an artist's client claiming that, since he has paid a million in commissioning the painting, he could also decide what color it has. This is a cultural misunderstanding. We regard it as completely normal to oppose a suggestion. I mean that the architect is not paid always to say 'yes', but rather to say 'no'. Otherwise, the client could simply recruit a couple of architectural draftsmen. Another example: you don't hire a shockingly expensive attorney for 1000 Marks an hour and on top of it explain to him the trial strategy. There you have to have a bit of confidence.

Keller / In this regard, architects have a better starting position. As a communications designer, I have to do a lot more convincing.

Ingenhoven / I believe that it is a question of openness, of a joint search for solutions. After all, we're only dealing with factual issues, not with love, hate and jealousy. Here it must be possible to make the required abstraction. And, as far as the relationship between client and architect is concerned, over time this is indeed subject to stress. At stake is not only the design, but also its realization. This is much more difficult, and above all it takes time. I would advise every client to scrutinize not only the design, but also the people who are to realize it. Take a project such as the reconstruction of the main station in Stuttgart. This extends over twelve years. For this period of time you have to live with each other. This is like a marriage.

Ingenhoven / Ich glaube, dass es eine Frage der Offenheit ist, der gemeinsamen Suche nach Lösungen. Es geht schließlich doch nur um sachliche Fragen, nicht etwa um Liebe, Hass und Eifersucht. Da muss es möglich sein, zu abstrahieren. Und was das Verhältnis zwischen Bauherrn und Architekten angeht, das ist über die Zeit durchaus einigen Belastungen ausgesetzt. Es geht nicht nur um den Entwurf, sondern auch darum, ihn zu realisieren. Das ist viel schwieriger, und vor allem dauert es seine Zeit. Ich würde jedem Auftraggeber raten, nicht nur den Entwurf zu prüfen, sondern auch die Menschen, die ihn verwirklichen sollen. Nehmen Sie ein Projekt wie den Umbau des Hauptbahnhofs in Stuttgart, das läuft über zwölf Jahre. So lange müssen sie es miteinander aushalten, das ist wie eine Ehe.

Keller / Das gilt auch im Design-Bereich, wenngleich die Zeiträume selten so groß sind (mit Ausnahmen: wir betreuen bereits seit zehn Jahren das Museum Villa Stuck). Der Vergleich mit Ehe und Partnerschaft ist sehr treffend, weil hier wie dort Vertrauen eine entscheidende Rolle spielt. Auch so etwas wie Nähe. Ich habe über den engen Kontakt mit dem Auftraggeber gesprochen: Das darf man nicht als lästige Begleiterscheinung abtun, das gehört dazu, sonst kann ich keine wirklich passende und dadurch überzeugende Gestaltung entwickeln. In dieser Phase geschieht es oft, dass ich »wir« sage und damit den Kunden und uns Designer als eine Einheit meine. Da gibt es im Vorstandsbereich befremdete Gesichter, aber es ist ein unbewusster Ausdruck dafür, wie tief wir uns in die Aufgabe hineinbegeben. Und da zählt jedes Detail.

Keller / This is also true of the area of design, even though the time periods involved are seldom this long (with exceptions: for ten years, we've been looking after the Villa Stuck museum). The comparison with marriage and partnership is very apt, since trust plays a crucial role in both cases. Something like closeness as well. I've talked about the close contact with the client: this must not be dismissed as an irksome concomitant. It is part of the work. Otherwise, I cannot develop a truly suitable and hence persuasive design. At this stage, I often say "we", thereby referring to the client and us designers as a unity. This provokes expressions of astonishment among members of the board, but t betrays how 'deeply' we delve into the task. And here every detail counts.

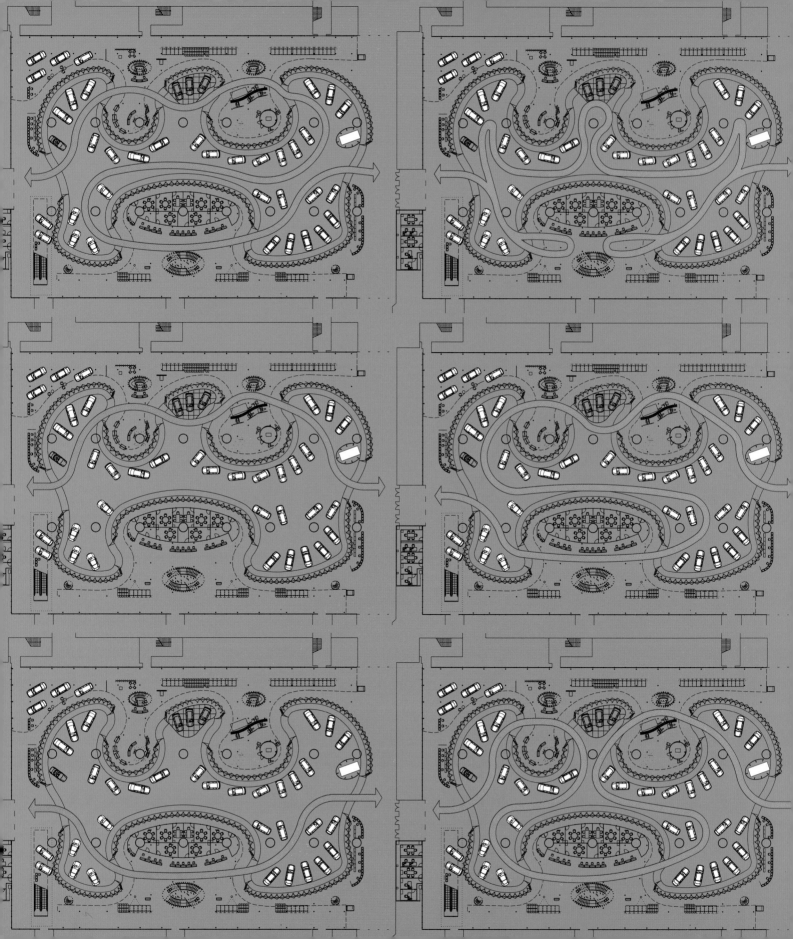

Detailfragen tauchen ja nicht nur in der Auseinandersetzung mit dem Auftraggeber auf. Was bedeutet es für Sie, ein Konzept bis ins letzte Detail auszuformen und ein Kommunikationsdesign aus einem Guss abzuliefern?

Keller / Ich will das mal an einem Beispiel erläutern. Als wir zur IAA 1997 für Audi erstmals einen Messeauftritt gestalteten, haben wir vom leeren Blatt Papier aus einen kompletten Entwurf hingelegt, ein neuartiges Kommunikationskonzept einschließlich Inszenierungen, Video-, Licht- und Musikdesign. Ein Detail haben wir jedoch außer Acht gelassen: das Standpersonal. Dafür war eine andere Abteilung zuständig, unsere Ansprechpartner hatten damit nichts zu tun, kurzum: Wie sich herausstellte, wurden die für die Messe engagierten Mitarbeiter nicht besonders gut bezahlt, hatten keine Einweisung bekommen und arbeiteten in einer einzigen Schicht. Noch dazu hatte man sie in der Jugendherberge untergebracht, um Hotelkosten zu sparen. Anders gesagt: Ihre Arbeitsbedingungen waren mies. Und das hat man ihnen nicht nur bald angesehen, das haben die Besucher letztlich auch zu spüren bekommen. Und wenn ich streng bin, ist unser schönes Gesamtkonzept daran gescheitert.

Questions of detail do not only come up in discussion with the client. What does it mean for you to shape a plan down to the last detail and submit a communications design as a completely rounded piece of work?

Keller / I want to illustrate this with an example. The first time we designed an exhibition for Audi at the International Auto Show in 1997, we laid down a complete design, starting from an empty sheet of paper. It was a new communications concept, including the staging of shows, video, lighting and music design. Yet, we ignored one detail: the personnel at the exhibition stand. Another department was responsible for this aspect. Our contacts at Audi had nothing to do with this. In short: as it turned out, the employees hired for the trade show were not paid particularly well, had not received any instruction and were working in a single shift. On top of it, they had been put up in the youth hostel, in order to save the costs for a hotel. In other words, their working conditions were terrible. Not only was it soon possible to tell this by looking at them; in the end, the visitors got to feel it as well. And, strictly speaking, our beautiful overall design failed because of it.

Ingenhoven / War das wirklich so schlimm?

Keller / Ja. Und daraus haben wir gelernt. Jetzt ist es so, dass die Crew Schulungen bekommt und eine aufwendig gestaltete Broschüre, in der nicht nur alles steht, was die Arbeit betrifft, sondern auch Tipps für Restaurants oder Diskotheken. Massagen werden angeboten, es gibt Preise für die beste Betreuung … und die Unterbringung erfolgt im Hotel: lauter Kleinigkeiten, die den stressigen Job angenehmer machen. Wer mal an die frische Luft will, kann sich abmelden, braucht nicht heimlich aufs Klo, um eine zu rauchen. Man kann viel darüber reden, wie man eine Unternehmensphilosophie gestaltet, letzten Endes hängt es oft an solchen Hilfestellungen für die Mitarbeiter. Solche Gesten haben eine große Bedeutung, denn die Menschen, an die sie sich richten, vertreten das Unternehmen.

Ist das Ihr Verständnis von Ganzheitlichkeit?

Keller / Unser Ziel ist immer eine Gesamtinszenierung. Dabei betrachten wir das Unternehmen oder die Institution als Einheit, als Ganzes – als ein Wesen, das Augen hat, das riecht, das Körperwärme hat, das zuhört und lebendig ist, mal lustig und mal traurig. Wir sehen es als unsere Aufgabe an, dieses Wesen wahrnehmbar, spürbar zu machen, egal, ob man uns nun das komplette Erscheinungsbild anvertraut oder nur einen Teilbereich: den Messeauftritt, die Website, die Geschäftsausstattung, den Geschäftsbericht oder vielleicht nur eine Broschüre.

Sie haben dafür den Begriff »Tiefendesign« geprägt. Passt diese Bezeichnung genauer auf ihr Selbstverständnis als »Corporate Design« oder »Kommunikationsdesign«?

Ingenhoven / Was it really that bad?

Keller / Yes. And we learnt our lesson. Now the crew receives training and an elaborate brochure, which contains not only all the details regarding work, but also tips for restaurants or dance clubs. Massages are offered, there are prizes for best customer care … and accommodation takes place in a hotel. These are all details that make a stressful job more pleasant. If people want some fresh air, they can sign out and don't secretly have to go to the washroom in order to smoke. Much can be said about designing a company philosophy, but in the end, it often depends on such measures of support for employees. Such gestures are very significant, because the people to whom they are addressed represent the company.

Is this your understanding of a holistic approach?

Keller / Our goal is always a holistic production. We consider the company or the institution as a unity, as a whole—as a being that has eyes, that smells, that has body heat, that listens and is alive, sometimes jovial and sometimes sad. We regard it as our task to make this being perceptible, noticeable—no matter, whether we are entrusted with the complete image or only a part of it: the trade show exhibit, the Website, the design of the store, the annual report or perhaps only a brochure.

You have coined the term "depth design" for this approach. Does this designation better suit your understanding of your work than "corporate design" or "communications design"?

Keller / Die letzteren Begriffe bezeichnen eher Tätigkeitsbereiche, während »Tiefendesign« sich auf die Art unseres Vorgehens bezieht. Wir schauen auf die Menschen, die in einem Unternehmen arbeiten, auf dessen Grundsätze und Strukturen sowie auf die Produkte, die erzeugt werden. Nur wenn man den Geist erfasst, die spezifische Atmosphäre, die all das zusammenhält, kann man etwas Lebendiges und Authentisches entwickeln. Wir arbeiten die Tiefenstrukturen heraus, um die passenden Ausdrucksmittel dafür zu finden.

Wann ist das der Fall?

Keller / Ob wir schließlich mit einer Arbeit zufrieden sind, hängt von ihrer inneren Logik ab. Die formale Kohärenz ist dafür ein guter Indikator, sozusagen an der Oberfläche. Ein ästhetisches Dogma aber gibt es für uns nicht. Es ist mittlerweile kein Zufall, dass die Unternehmen gerade dann bei uns anfragen, wenn es um ihre grundsätzliche Stellung, um ihre Identität geht. Unsere Schwerpunkte liegen deshalb in solchen Aufgaben, die mit dem Wesen eines Unternehmens oder einer Einrichtung stark verbunden sind. Das sind klassischerweise Markenentwicklung und Corporate Design, aber auch Geschäftsberichte, und ganz besonders haben Messen, Ausstellungen und die Gestaltung des Firmensitzes mit der Identität des Unternehmens zu tun, denn hier geht es um die direkte, physische Begegnung.

Sie geben den Firmen also ein neues Profil?

Keller / The latter terms designate rather fields of activity, while "depth design" refers to our approach. We look at the people who work at a company. We look at the company's principles and structures as well as at the products it produces. Only when you have grasped the spirit, the specific atmosphere that holds everything together, can you develop something that is alive and authentic. We work out the deep structures, in order to find the suitable means of expressing them.

When is this the case?

Keller / Whether in the end we are satisfied with a piece of work depends on its inner logic. Formal coherence is a good indicator for this, at the surface, so to speak. An aesthetic dogma, however, does not exist for us. By now it is no accident that companies approach us especially when it concerns their fundamental position, their identity. This is why we are mainly focused on tasks that are strongly tied to the essential character of a company or institution. Classically, these are brand development and corporate design, but also annual reports. But especially trade fairs, exhibitions and the design of the headquarters are bound up with the identity of the company, since here we are dealing with the direct, physical encounter.

Keller / Wir schaffen keine Identitäten, sondern arbeiten das Vorhandene und möglicherweise Verborgene heraus. Eine kleine Geschichte dazu: Als ich in New York studierte, wohnte ich in einem Appartmentbau auf einer Etage mit einem Salvadorianer. Der hatte im Gegensatz zu mir einen Fernseher und ließ mich TV schauen im Tausch gegen Zeichnungen, die ich für ihn machte. Das konnte ich damals sehr gut. Einmal sollte ich ein Porträt von ihm zeichnen, das er seiner Mutter zu Weihnachten schenken wollte. Es sollte besonders schön werden, und er bat mich, ich möge seine Nase ein bisschen europäischer machen, den Hals ein bisschen länger, die Haare kürzer und ordentlicher. Ich führte das alles artig aus und brachte ihm das Bild. »Das bin nicht ich«, sagte er, und aus dem Fernsehen wurde nichts. Ich habe daraus gelernt. Gestaltung hat keinen Wert, wenn sie nicht authentisch ist.

Does this mean that you give companies a new profile?

Keller / We do not create identities, but rather work out what already exists
and is possibly hidden. I have a little story on this: when I was studying in New
York, I lived in an apartment building with a Salvadorian as a neighbor on my
floor. Unlike me, he had a television set and would let me watch in exchange for
drawings that I would make for him. I was very good at this at the time. Once,
I was supposed to draw a portrait of him, which he wanted to give to his mother
for Christmas. He wanted the portrait to be especially beautiful, and he asked
me to make his nose a bit more European, his neck a little longer, the hair short-
er and better groomed. I dutifully did as I was told and brought him the picture.
"This is not me", he said, and then there was no more television. I've learnt from
this. Design has no value, if it isn't authentic.

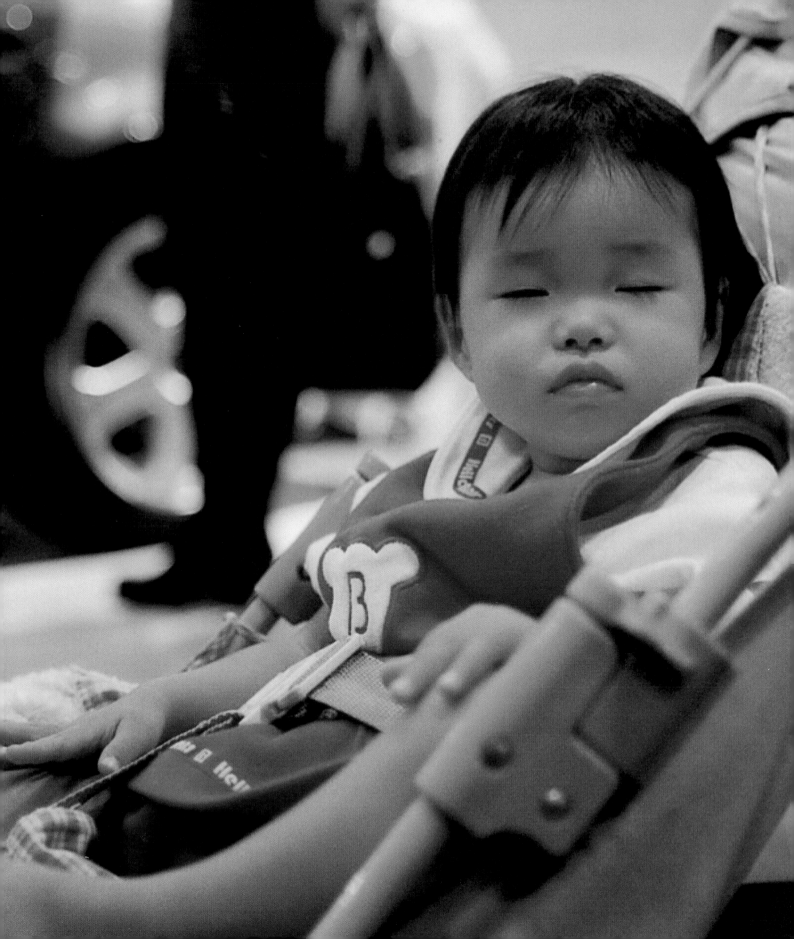

L'avenir c'est

Zukunft ist

Bien fu

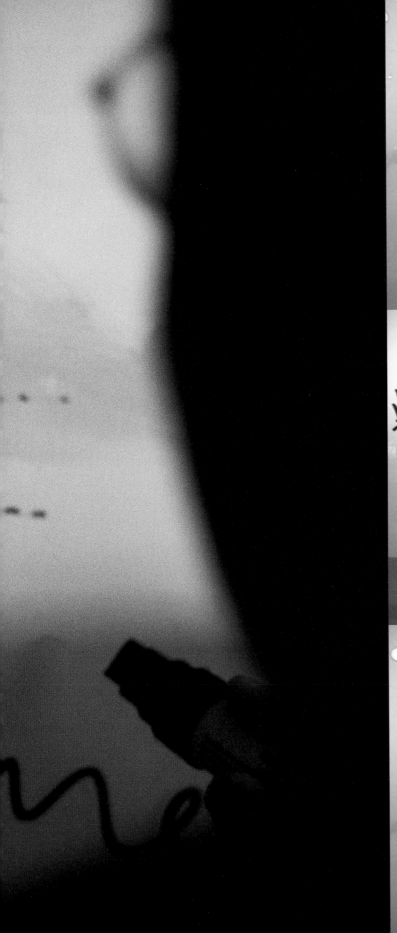

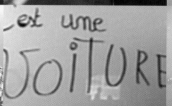

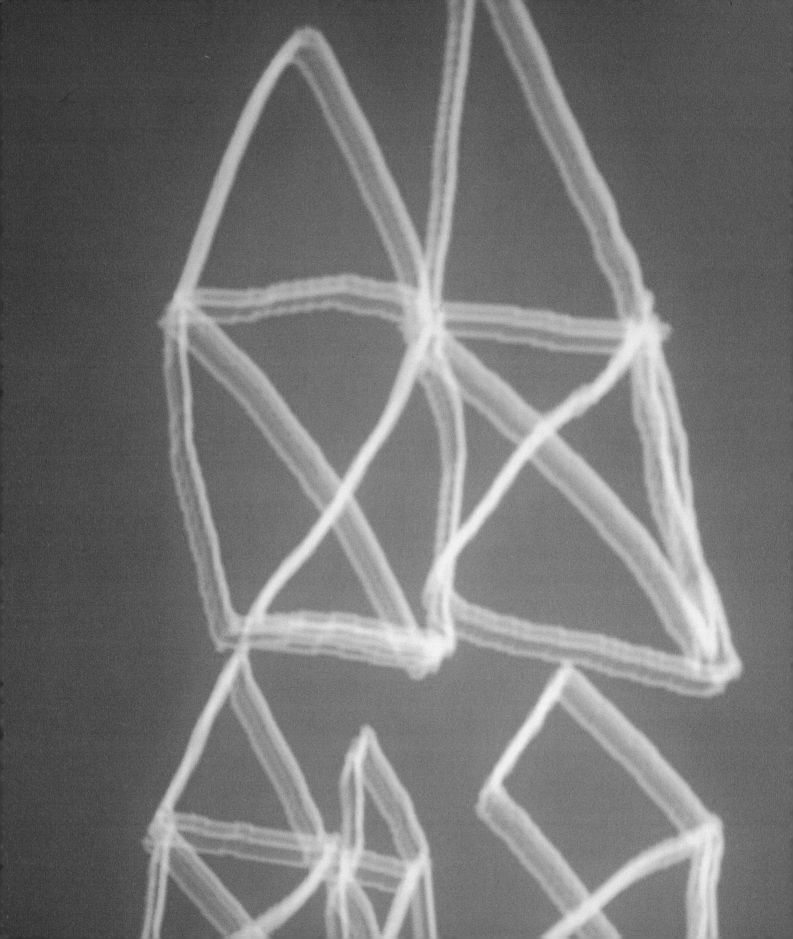

Audi Kids Club

TARTE AUX FRUITS
BOULE DE BERLIN
TARTE AU CITRON

HENNIEZ GAZ, NAT. & LÉGÈRE
FONTE LIMPIA
SAN PELLEGRINO
COCA-COLA, COCA LIGHT
SPRITE, FANTA, RIVELLA
JUS DE POMMES, SINALCO
JUS D'ORANGE, TOMATE
NECTAR DE GRAPEFRUIT
SCHWEPPES
THÉ FROID
BIÈRE SANS ALCOOL
CARDINAL SPÉCIALE
CARDINAL DRAFT
HEINEKEN
CAFÉ, THÉ, INFUSIONS

Bleiben wir bei der schillernden Vokabel »Ganzheitlichkeit«. Herr Ingenhoven, Sie sind bekannt geworden als Architekt von Öko-Hochhäusern. Vielleicht können Sie daran Ihre Vorstellung des Begriffes erläutern.

Ingenhoven / Der Begriff hat seinen Sinn, so inflationär er manchmal auch gebraucht wird. Er sagt, dass pures Spezialistentum, dass das reine Addieren partikularer Teile zu kurz greift. Wenn sich das Spektrum eines Architekten auf Hochhäuser reduzierte, hieße das, dass er keinen ganzheitlichen Anspruch hat. An der Konstruktion von Hochhäusern nur das Ökologische wahrzunehmen, ist ebenfalls zu wenig. Unsere Entwürfe haben eine ganze Menge wichtiger Eigenschaften, die wenig mit Ökologie und energiesparender Architektur zu tun haben. Obgleich dieser Aspekt natürlich an ihnen sehr wichtig ist, so wichtig meinetwegen wie Konstruktion, Räumlichkeit, Schönheit und die Förderung sozialer Beziehungen.

Woran können Sie den Begriff Ganzheitlichkeit dann festmachen?

Ingenhoven / Ich würde ihn als Anspruch so definieren: Architektur hilft den Menschen zu leben und zu überleben. Wenn das, was wir entwerfen, nicht das Leben erleichtert und verbessert, nicht das Arbeiten richtiger, schöner, angenehmer macht, dann haben wir unseren Job verfehlt. Das haben alle unsere Projekte gemeinsam, ob es nun der Stuttgarter Hauptbahnhof, die Hochhäuser oder der Messestand ist.

Sie sind also kein Vertreter von »sexy architecture« …

Let's stay with the dazzling term "holistic approach". Mr. Ingenhoven, you've made your name as an architect of eco-high-rise buildings. Perhaps you can explain your idea of this concept with reference to this type of architecture.

Ingenhoven / The concept has its sense despite the fact that the word is over-used. It says that pure specialist professionalism, the mere adding of particular parts, falls short. If the spectrum of an architect were reduced to high-rise buildings, this would mean that he has no holistic claim. It is also not enough merely to perceive the ecological aspect in the construction of high-rises. Our designs have a great many important characteristics that have little to do with ecology and energy-saving architecture. Although this aspect, of course, is very important in them—as important, for instance, as construction, spatial design, beauty and the promotion of social relations.

With respect to what can the concept of a "holistic approach" then be explained.

Ingenhoven / I would define its claim in the following manner: architecture helps people live and survive. If what we design does not facilitate and improve life, if it does not make people's work better, nicer and more pleasant, we have failed in our job. This is common to all our projects, whether it is the Stuttgart main station, the high-rises or the trade show stand.

It seems you are no advocate of "sexy architecture"…

Ingenhoven / Ich halte den Begriff für blanken Unsinn. Nicht die Architektur evoziert die Gefühle, sie schafft den Rahmen, in dem Gefühle möglich werden. Und Architektur ist nun mal ein sehr bestimmender Teil unseres Lebens. Man hält sich praktisch zu 100 Prozent seiner Zeit in einer bebauten Umwelt auf. Es ist selten im Leben eines Mitteleuropäers, dass er nicht mit Architektur konfrontiert ist. Das heißt auch, dass Architekten eine große Verantwortung tragen, der sie leider viel zu oft nicht gerecht werden.

Architektur erfülle dann ihren Anspruch, haben Sie gesagt, wenn sie das Leben und Arbeiten ermöglicht, für das sie gebaut ist. Für Burda in Offenburg haben Sie ein Bürohaus gebaut, das den kommunikativen Aspekt der Arbeit betont. Nach welchen Prinzipien sind Sie da vorgegangen?

Ingenhoven / Die Welt der Büroarbeit ist im Wandel begriffen. Sie ist offener, freier und transparenter geworden. Die abgeschlossene Welt der eiskalten Konzernzentralen ist passé. Auch wenn es immer noch weitgehend die Schreibtischarbeit am Computer ist, so wird doch die direkte Kommunikation wiederentdeckt. Dafür braucht man adäquate Räume, hoch genug, schön genug, mit guter Beleuchtung und guter Atmosphäre. Es können neutrale Hüllen sein, mit einer neuen Form der Landschaftlichkeit, mit tief gestaffelten und mehrgeschossigen Räumen, die echte Räume sind und keine Schuhschachteln. Und es müssen Räume mit Identität sein, die auch so manche Nutzungsänderung überstehen. Denn es steht zu erwarten, dass Büroorganisation und Arbeitseinheiten in Zukunft wohl immer flüchtiger werden. Diese stärkere Flexibilität von Gebäuden ist eine Form von Nachhaltigkeit, weil sie sich dauerhafter nutzen lassen. Das haben wir bei Burda verwirklicht.

Wird denn diese neue Offenheit auch von den Mitarbeitern angenommen?

Ingenhoven / I consider this concept to be sheer nonsense. Architecture does not evoke feelings, it creates the framework, in which feelings become possible. And architecture, after all, is a very determining aspect of our lives. Practically 100 percent of our time is spent in a built-up environment. It happens very seldom in the life of a Central European that he's not confronted with architecture. This also means that architects bear a great responsibility, which, unfortunately, they much too often fail to fulfill.

You said that architecture would fulfill its claim, if it made possible the life and work for which it is built. In Offenburg, you have built an office building for Burda that emphasizes the communicative aspect of work. According to what principles did you proceed in this case?

Ingenhoven / The world of office work is changing. It has become more open, free and transparent. The closed-off world of the ice-cold corporate headquarters is passé. Even if to a large extent deskwork at the computer prevails, direct communication is nevertheless being rediscovered. For this purpose you need adequate rooms, sufficiently high, sufficiently beautiful, with good lighting and good atmosphere. These can be neutral shells with a new sense of landscape, with deeply staggered and multi-storied rooms that are genuine rooms and not shoe boxes. And they must be rooms with an identity, which can also survive a few changes in use. For it is to be expected that in the future office organization and work units will become more and more fleeting. This increased flexibility of buildings is a form of sustainability, because they can be used for a longer term. And this is what we achieved at Burda.

Ingenhoven / Es bedarf immer einiger Überzeugungskraft, wenn jemand das aufgeben soll, was er gewohnt ist. Bei Burda haben wir zusammen mit externen Beratern eine Reihe von Workshops mit den Mitarbeitern durchgeführt, um uns ein Bild von ihren Bedürfnissen und den Erfordernissen der Arbeit zu machen. Wir haben dann die Tätigkeiten aus allen Häusern auf dem Burda-Gelände sortiert und dafür gesorgt, dass die Trennung nach erscheinenden Titeln aufgehoben wird und dafür die Gruppierung nach affinen Tätigkeiten erfolgt: Redakteure, Anzeigenverwaltung, Reinzeichner etc. Ich fahre heute sehr gerne hin, denn das Ergebnis ist fast besser, als wir gedacht haben. Man sieht, dass das Haus funktioniert.

Sie haben in mehreren Interviews ein klares Bekenntnis zur Moderne abgelegt. Jetzt wollen Sie, wenn ich Sie richtig interpretiere, die Zumutungen der postindustriellen Arbeitswelt abschwächen. Liegt darin nicht eine gewisse Ungleichzeitigkeit?

Ingenhoven / Die Moderne ist für mich kein Stil, und sie steht für mich deswegen nicht für eine abgeschlossene Epoche. In einer Welt, die zunehmend disparater wird, in der es den Steinzeitmenschen neben Individuen geben wird, die dauerhaft in einer Raumstation leben, werden Fragen nach einem Stil hinfällig. Mich interessiert die Moderne in ganz anderer Hinsicht: als ein Projekt, das in der Aufklärung seinen vorläufigen Höhepunkt hatte, aber längst nicht endet. Sie bedeutet Erkenntnis, Wissen, Emanzipation von überkommenen religiösen, dogmatischen und ideologischen ›Verklebungen‹. Und sie lässt sich nicht durch Fundamentalismus oder Postmoderne beenden. Das Menschheitsprojekt der Moderne hat seine eigene Geschichte und seine eigenen Gesetze. Wir können es nicht aufhalten, wir können es behindern oder befördern. Ich jedenfalls bin ein unbedingter Verfechter des Beförderns.

Is this new openness also accepted by the employees?

Ingenhoven / A certain persuasiveness is always required, when people are to give up what they are accustomed to. At Burda, we conducted with the help of external consultants a series of workshops with the employees, in order to gain an idea of their needs and the requirements of their work. We then sorted the activities from all of the buildings on the Burda premises and ensured that the separation according to displayed titles is abolished and a grouping according to related activities is introduced: editing, advertising administration, fair drawing etc. Today, I really enjoy going there, because the result is almost better than we thought. One can see that the building works.

In several interviews, you have made a clear avowal of your commitment to modernity. Now, if I interpret you correctly, you want to mitigate the impositions of the post-industrial world of work. Does this not harbor a certain non-synchronicity?

Welchen Anteil hat die Architektur daran?

Ingenhoven / Was wir gemeinhin unter Moderne verstehen, war bestenfalls das künstlerische Nachvollziehen einer Entwicklung, die in der Welt der Ingenieure längst vollzogen war. Die Fließbandproduktion bei Ford und die Erfindung der Dampfmaschine waren um vieles revolutionärer als alles, was Le Corbusier jemals gebaut hat. Wenn Architekten sich heute für die Speerspitze des Fortschritts halten, hat das möglicherweise mit einer Form von Unwissen zu tun. Und wenn sie meinen, für ihre Konstruktionen ein besonders avanciertes Computerprogramm zu verwenden, und daraus eine Sensation machen, denke ich, sie müssen die vergangenen 20 Jahre geschlafen haben. Denn ähnliche Programme hat die Autoindustrie seit nahezu 30 Jahren eingesetzt, völlig selbstverständlich, aus schlichter Notwendigkeit.

Warum sollten Architektur und Kommunikationsdesign auch weiterhin Partnerschaften schließen?

Ingenhoven / Weil man diese Aufgaben schlicht nicht denen überlassen darf, die es falsch machen. Denen, die schlechte Multiplex-Kinos, noch schlechtere Einkaufszentren und fürchterliche Tankstellen bauen. Der Architekt wird da allzu schnell zum Anhängsel des ›Shopping Center Designers‹. Was dabei herauskommt, kann man ja überall besichtigen. Man muss die Kooperation üben und sich darauf einlassen. Sonst stellt der Architekt ein Gebäude hin und fällt dann aus allen Wolken, weil anschließend der ›Attraction Designer‹ kommt und das Haus verschandelt …

Ingenhoven / For me, modernity is not a style and hence does not stand for an era that has ended. In a world that is becoming increasingly disparate, in which we will have stone-age people alongside individuals, who permanently inhabit a space station, questions concerning a style lose their validity. Modernity interests me in a completely different regard: as a project that reached its provisional peak in the Enlightenment, but is nowhere close to ending. It signifies cognition, knowledge, emancipation from traditional religious, dogmatic and ideological 'entanglements'. And it cannot be ended through fundamentalism or post-modernism. The project of humanity that is modernity has its own history and its own laws. We cannot stop it, we can only impede or promote it. I, for my part, am an unconditional advocate of its promotion.

What part does architecture have in this?

Ingenhoven / What we commonly understand as modernity was at best the artistic reconstruction of a development that had long been completed in the world of the engineers. The assembly line production at Ford and the invention of the steam turbine were more revolutionary by far than anything Le Corbusier has ever built. When architects today take themselves to be the spearhead of progress, this possibly has something to do with a form of ignorance. And when they believe that they are using a particularly advanced computer program for their constructions and turn this into a sensation, I think that they must have been sleeping during the last 20 years. Because similar programs have been used in the auto industry for almost 30 years, quite naturally, out of sheer necessity.

Keller / Es geht auch um die Qualität der Auseinandersetzung. Wenn mein Gegenüber mich fordert, wird das Projekt zu einer Bereicherung für mich – und umgekehrt genauso. Abgesehen vom konkreten Ergebnis der Zusammenarbeit werden bei jedem Beteiligten neue Perspektiven eröffnet und Energien freigesetzt. So trägt jeder einen neuen Impuls in die Welt hinein.

Kommen wir zum Schluss nochmals auf den Begriff »Zukunft« zurück. Zählt er heutzutage wieder, oder muss man in ihm nur eine leere Worthülse sehen? Gibt es so etwas wie eine Aufbruchstimmung?

Ingenhoven / Natürlich gibt es wieder eine Aufbruchstimmung. Ich finde es im Übrigen fast schon tröstlich, dass das Wort »Zukunft« wieder zählt, auch wenn es inflationär gebraucht wird. Es gibt jedenfalls ein enormes Interesse an neuen Technologien. Ich liebe den Blick des Ingenieurs auf die Welt. Ich glaube nicht an die Haltung des Philosophen.

Keller / Für mich ist Gestaltung immer auch Philosophie. Paul Renner, Bodoni, Frutiger oder Otl Aicher haben ihre Weltanschauung und damit auch ihre Zeit zum Ausdruck gebracht. Jeder Gedanke nimmt früher oder später Gestalt an, deshalb wird es stets auch Design geben. Ich bin davon überzeugt, dass das Design der Zukunft in einer viel philosophischeren Herangehensweise an die Dinge bestehen wird.

Ingenhoven / Was, glauben Sie, hat das Leben mehr beeinflusst: die Mondlandung oder Picasso? Ich neige generell dazu zu sagen, dass das Sein das Bewusstsein bestimmt, nicht umgekehrt. Ich glaube einfach an die Macht von Natur und Technik. Ich glaube daran, dass das Erkennenwollen und die Erkenntnis unser Leben bestimmen.

Why should architecture and communications design continue to form partnerships?

Ingenhoven / Because we simply must not leave these tasks to those who do things the wrong way. To those who build bad multiplex cinemas, even worse shopping centers and terrible gas stations. In those contexts, the architect very quickly turns into an appendage of the 'shopping center designer'. The results can be seen everywhere. Instead, we must practice cooperation and get involved in it. Otherwise, the architect will put up a building and then be flabbergasted, when the 'attraction designer' comes and spoils it…

Keller / The quality of the discussion is also a factor. If I am challenged by my counterpart, the project will be enriching for me—and vice versa. Aside from the concrete product of the cooperation, new perspectives are opened for every participant and energies are released. And in this way, everyone carries a new impulse into the world.

Let us return in conclusion once more to the concept of the "future". Does it mean something again today, or must one regard it merely as an empty cliché? Is there really a sense of the beginning of something new?

Ingenhoven / Of course, there is again a sense of beginning something new. By the way, I already find it almost comforting that the word "future" counts for something again, even if it is overused. There is in any case an enormous interest in new technologies. I love the way the engineer looks upon the world. I don't believe in the attitude of the philosopher.

Keller / Ohne Picasso könnte ich nicht leben, weil er mir das Gefühl gibt, da sei noch mehr, eine ganze Welt, die er mir eröffnen kann. Und die Mondlandung? Klar, die begreife ich, Technik fasziniert mich auch. Aber je älter ich werde, desto mehr lasse ich mich von Dingen berühren, die sich mir nicht sofort formal oder technisch erschließen. Eine Kathedrale zum Beispiel. Würde sie uns ergreifen, wenn sie einfach nur ein großes Gebäude wäre? Wenn sie nicht mit der Religiosität aufgeladen wäre, die darin zelebriert wird? Wenn es nicht die Stille, die Andacht gäbe, die darin herrscht?

Ingenhoven / Ich glaube doch. Ich glaube, dass die Architektur uns ergreift und nicht eine Idee. Ich glaube, die Architektur ermöglicht uns erst, diese Idee überhaupt zu denken. In den schönsten Momenten kann Architektur das ausstrahlen, was sonst nur die Natur vermag. Und das ist im Übrigen auch das Beste, was man über jede Art von Kunst sagen kann. Die Architektur muss sich messen lassen an einem Landschaftserlebnis. Ich steige auf den Mont Blanc und schaue hinunter auf die Wolken, ins Tal. Diese Stille, diese Schönheit, das ist die Konkurrenz für mich als Architekten.

Keller / For me, design is also philosophy. Paul Renner, Bodoni, Frutiger or Otl Aicher have given expression to their view of the world and hence also to their time. Sooner or later, every thought takes on a form, and this is why there will always be design. I am convinced that the design of the future will consist in a much more philosophical approach to things.

Ingenhoven / What do you believe has influenced life more profoundly: man's landing on the moon or Picasso? I generally tend towards the view that being determines consciousness and not the other way around. I simply believe in the power of nature and technology. I believe that cognition and the desire for knowledge determine our lives.

Keller / I could not live without Picasso, because he gives me the feeling that there is still more, a whole world, which he could disclose to me. And the landing on the moon? Sure, I understand it. Technology fascinates me too. But the older I get, the more I allow myself be touched by things that are not immediately accessible to me in a formal or technical way. A cathedral, for example. Would it move us, if it were merely a large building? If it weren't laden with die religiosity that is celebrated in it? If the silence, the devotion that reign within it didn't exist?

Ingenhoven / I believe so. I believe that it is the architecture that moves us and not an idea. I believe that the architecture first makes it possible for us to think this idea at all. In the most beautiful moments, architecture can communicate what is otherwise only within nature's power. And, besides, this is the best thing one can say about any type of art. Architecture must allow itself to be judged by comparison with the experience of a landscape. I climb Mont Blanc and look down upon the clouds, into the valley. This silence, this beauty, this is the competition for me as an architect.

Anhang / Appendix

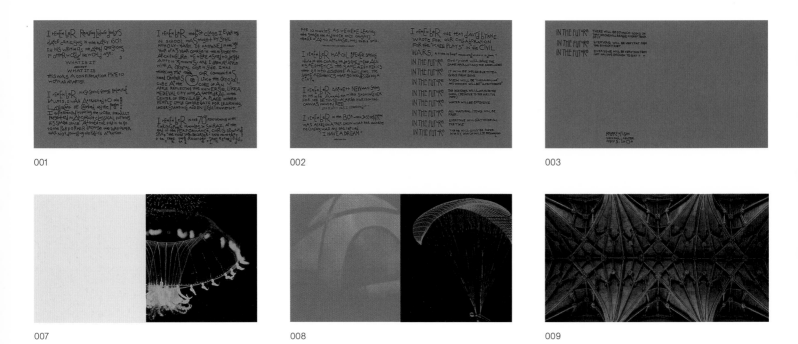

001 002 003

007 008 009

001 to 003 Original essay by Robert M. Wilson for "1/1". During a drive from Oberammergau to Füssen in May 2000—one day before the opening of Wilson's installation, "Stations of the Cross", which ran parallel to the Passion plays—Michael Keller told the American director and pioneer of interdisciplinary design about this book project and asked him for a contribution. **004 to 006** Nguyen Minh, who came to Germany 22 years ago from Saigon, is the owner of the restaurant "Orchid", near the former premises of KMS Design in Munich. When asked about the reason for his smile, the frequency of which is conspicuous even in the context of Far Eastern politeness, he said: "My smile prompts most people to smile back. Thus I'm surrounded all day by cheerful faces". The affinity of this attitude to the basic ideas of communications design regarding the role of a host made Nguyen Minh a sort of allegorical figure of the holistic approach. **007 to 013** Illustrative motifs from the presentation by Ingenhoven Overdiek und Partner during competition. "For the participation at the competition, we had received a briefing from KMS, which stated two central requirements: the architecture was supposed to create a self-contained logical world … And it was supposed to be a light and transparent piece of work …" [Christoph Ingenhoven] **007** Jellyfish of the class hydrozoa hydroidomedus. "The evolutionary process of living beings and plants can be the determining guide for architects and engineers." [Christoph Ingenhoven, in: Evolution Ökologie Architektur, Aedes 1996] **008** Left: Self-supporting lightweight tent in the shape of an igloo. Right: Computer model for the optimization of material efficiency—paraglider. The stated goal was to develop an efficient and self-supporting structure for the space-creating elements of the exhibition stand. "A central task in the planning process is to achieve more with less, to generate a higher utility value from a lower consumption of resources." [Christoph Ingenhoven in: Evolution Ökologie Architektur, Aedes 1996] **009** Nave of the Winchester Cathedral in Hampshire. "Architecture is well suited for conveying emotionality. A Gothic cathedral does this by enveloping the visitor with its grandiose spatiality. At the same time, we decided to tackle the topic of construction. It is true that we wanted to create a world that speaks to feelings—but we wanted to design it with the rational and technical means of engineers." [Christoph Ingenhoven] **010** Left: Deformed microfiber. Right: Acer Palmatum Japonica [Japanese maple]. In a first sketch of ideas it was already decided that images of nature, continually changing throughout the day, such as moving clouds, underwater images, wheat fields or deciduous trees in the wind but also microstructures should be projected onto the space-creating structure of the exhibition stand. **011** Left: Hydromechanical structure—wave. Right: The yacht "Crazy Horse", sail number US 87219. Nature and technology, power and lightness were the essential parameters of design. For its implementation, materials used in high-performance sports were analyzed in terms of their properties and the manner in which they are joined. The results served as a benchmark for all of the structural solutions that had yet to be developed. **012** Left: Growth process of a colony of Proteus bacteria. Right: Sand dune in the Sahara. The spatial continuum of the exhibition space was to extend into a vast landscape.

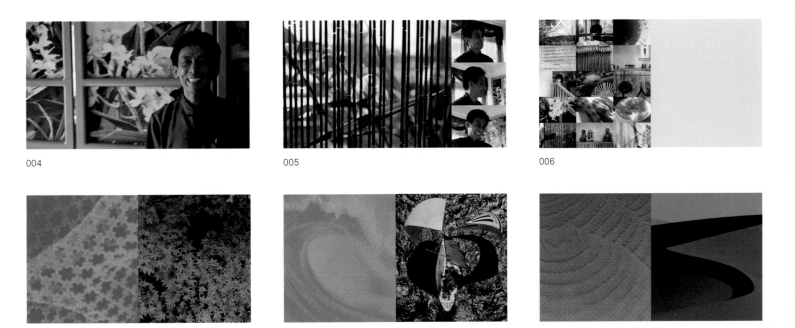

004 005 006

010 011 012

001 bis 003 Originalessay von Robert M. Wilson für »1/1«. Auf einer Autofahrt von Oberammergau nach Füssen im Mai 2000, am Tag vor der Eröffnung von Wilsons Kreuzweg-Installation, die parallel zu den Passionsspielen zu sehen war, erzählte Michael Keller dem amerikanischen Regisseur von diesem Buchprojekt und bat ihn, als einen der Pioniere interdisziplinären Gestaltens, um einen Beitrag. 004 bis 006 Nguyen Minh aus Saigon, seit 22 Jahren in Deutschland, Inhaber des Restaurants »Orchid« in der Nähe der vormaligen Räume von KMS in München. Gefragt nach dem Grund für sein auch im Rahmen fernöstlicher Höflichkeit auffällig häufiges Lachen, sagte er: »Mein Lachen führt dazu, dass die meisten Leute zurücklachen. So bin ich den ganzen Tag von fröhlichen Gesichtern umgeben.« Die Affinität dieser Haltung zu den Grundgedanken des Kommunikationsdesigns über die Bedeutung der Gastgeberrolle machten Nguyen Minh zu einer Art allegorischen Figur des ganzheitlichen Vorgehens. 007 bis 013 Bildmotive aus der Wettbewerbspräsentation, Ingenhoven Overdiek und Partner. »Für die Teilnahme am Wettbewerb hatten wir von KMS ein Briefing erhalten, aus dem zwei zentrale Anforderungen hervorgingen: Die Architektur sollte eine in sich geschlossene logische Welt schaffen. … Und es sollte eine leichte, transparente Arbeit sein …« [Christoph Ingenhoven] 007 Qualle aus der Klasse der Hydrozoa Hydroidomedus. »Der Evolutionsprozess der Lebewesen und Pflanzen kann der bestimmende Ratgeber für Architekten und Ingenieure sein.« [Christoph Ingenhoven, in: Evolution Ökologie Architektur, Aedes 1996] 008 Links: Selbsttragendes Leichtgewichtzelt, Igluform. Rechts: Computermodell zur Optimierung der Materialeffizienz, Paraglider. Es war das formulierte Ziel, eine effiziente und selbsttragende Konstruktion für die raumbildenden Elemente des Messestandes zu entwickeln. »Mit weniger mehr zu erreichen, aus geringerem Ressourcenverbrauch mehr Nutzwert zu generieren ist eine zentrale Aufgabe im Planungsprozess.« [Christoph Ingenhoven, in: Evolution Ökologie Architektur, Aedes 1996] 009 Langhaus der Kathedrale von Winchester, Hampshire. »Architektur hat gute Chancen, Emotionalität zu transportieren. Eine gotische Kathedrale tut dies, indem sie den Besucher mit ihrer grandiosen Räumlichkeit umfängt. Gleichzeitig haben wir uns entschieden, das Thema Konstruktion anzugehen. Zwar wollten wir eine Welt schaffen, die die Gefühle anspricht – aber wir wollten sie mit den rationalen und technischen Mitteln des Ingenieurs entwerfen.« [Christoph Ingenhoven] 010 Links: Verformte Mikrofaser. Rechts: Acer Palmatum Japonica [japan. Spitz- oder Fächerahorn]. Bereits in einer ersten Ideenskizze stand fest, dass auf die raumbildende Konstruktion des Messestandes über den Tagesverlauf sich kontinuierlich verändernde Naturbilder, wie ziehende Wolken, Unterwasserbilder, Weizenfelder oder Laubbäume im Wind, aber auch Mikrostrukturen projiziert werden sollten. 011 Links: Hydromechanische Struktur, Welle. Rechts: Segelyacht »Crazy Horse«, Segelnummer US 87219. Natur und Technik, Kraft und Leichtigkeit waren die wesentlichen Entwurfsparameter. Für die Umsetzung wurden Materialien aus dem Hochleistungssport sowie deren Eigenschaften und Fügungen analysiert. An dieser Benchmark mussten sich alle noch zu entwickelnden Konstruktionslösungen messen lassen. 012 Links: Wachstumsprozess einer Proteus-Bakterienkolonie. Rechts: Sanddüne in der Sahara. Das Raumkontinuum des Ausstellungsraumes sollte sich zu einer weitläufigen Landschaft ausdehnen.

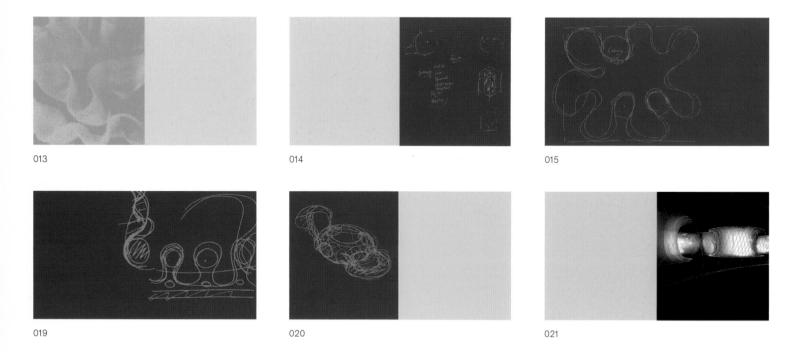

013   014   015

019   020   021

013 Nest of eggs of a tropical sea slug [Nudi Branchia] **014** Christoph Ingenhoven, design sketch for the 1998 competition. "We had in mind the principle of the Laterna Magica—at a technologically demanding level, of course—in order to intimate something like the course of a day." [Christoph Ingenhoven] **015** Christoph Ingenhoven, design sketch for the 1998 competition. "The starting point was the idea of creating a world. A world, I always imagine as something enveloping, something closed. In the womb. Under water. Or when I'm lying in a field of wheat and the ears close up above me. There is a continuum of surfaces. The dimensions have no clear-cut dividing lines. These considerations gave rise to a simple sketch, an amoebic form, which already contained many crucial aspects." [Christoph Ingenhoven] **016** Christoph Ingenhoven, design sketch for the IAA Frankfurt, 1998 competition. »loop [luːp] [= *curved shape*] Schlaufe *f*; [*of wire*] Schlinge *f*; [*of river, Rail*] Schleife *f*; [*Med*] Spirale *f*; to knock or throw sb for a ~ [*esp US inf*] jdn völlig umhauen [*inf*]; [*Aviat*] Looping *m*; to ~ the ~ einen Looping machen; [*Comput*] Schleife *f*« [Collins: german-english english-german, Pons-Großwörterbuch] **017** Christoph Ingenhoven, design sketch for the TMS Tokyo Motor Show 1999 **018 and 019** Christoph Ingenhoven, design sketches for the Paris Motor Show 2000 **020** Christoph Ingenhoven, design sketch for the TMS Tokyo Motor Show 1999. **021 and 022** Grid model of the exhibition space, 1998 competition. The first three-dimensional implementations already revealed the spatial qualities of the architecture of the exhibition stand: All of the spatial enclosures were essentially defined and were later, in the course of further revision, adjusted to actual requirements. **023** Computer simulation of the 'loop', 1998 competition. The three-dimensional computer model of the grid structures formed the basis of all further plans and calculations. Only because of the early and precise conversion into drawings and 3D models was it possible to adhere to the short time frame. **024** Presentational model for the IAA Frankfurt, 1998 competition. The qualities of the interior space were verified by means of models constructed to scale [1:87].

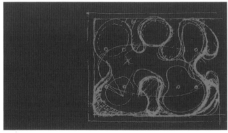

016

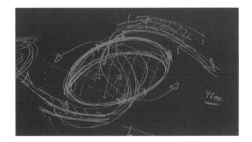

017

018

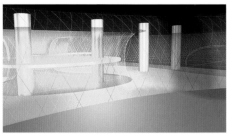

022

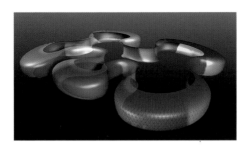

023

024

013 Gelege einer tropischen Meeresnacktschnecke [Nudi Branchia]. **014** Christoph Ingenhoven, Entwurfsskizze Wettbewerb 1998. »Wir hatten das Prinzip der Laterna magica im Sinn, natürlich auf technisch anspruchsvollem Niveau, um so etwas wie einen Tagesablauf anzudeuten.« [Christoph Ingenhoven] **015** Christoph Ingenhoven, Entwurfsskizze Wettbewerb 1998. »Ausgangspunkt war der Gedanke, eine Welt zu schaffen. Unter einer Welt stelle ich mir etwas Umhüllendes, etwas Geschlossenes vor. Im Mutterleib. Unter Wasser. Oder wenn ich in einem Weizenfeld liege und die Ähren über mir zusammenfallen. Es gibt ein Kontinuum der Oberflächen, die Dimensionen haben fließende Übergänge. Aus diesen Überlegungen entstand eine simple Skizze, eine amöbenähnliche Form, die bereits viele entscheidende Aspekte beinhaltete.« [Christoph Ingenhoven] **016** Christoph Ingenhoven, Entwurfsskizze IAA Frankfurt, Wettbewerb 1998. »loop [luːp] [= *curved shape*] Schlaufe *f*; [*of wire*] Schlinge *f*; [*of river, Rail*] Schleife *f*; [*Med*] Spirale *f*; to knock or throw sb for a ~ [*esp US inf*] jdn völlig umhauen [*inf*]; [*Aviat*] Looping *m*; to ~ the ~ einen Looping machen; [*Comput*] Schleife *f*« [Collins: deutsch-englisch englisch-deutsch, Pons-Großwörterbuch] **017** Christoph Ingenhoven, Entwurfsskizze TMS Tokyo Motor Show 1999. **018 und 019** Christoph Ingenhoven, Entwurfsskizzen Mondial de l'Automobile Paris 2000. **020** Christoph Ingenhoven, Entwurfsskizze TMS Tokyo Motor Show 1999. **021 und 022** Gittermodell Ausstellungsraum, Wettbewerb 1998. Bereits die ersten dreidimensionalen Ausarbeitungen zeigten die räumlichen Qualitäten der Standarchitektur. Alle bespielbaren Raumabschlüsse waren im Wesentlichen definiert und wurden später an die realen Erfordernisse angepasst. **023** Computersimulation ›Loop‹, Wettbewerb 1998. Das dreidimensionale Computermodell der Gitterstrukturen war Grundlage aller weiteren Planungen und Berechnungen. Nur durch die frühzeitige und präzise Umsetzung in Zeichnungen und 3-D-Modelle konnte der kurze Zeitrahmen eingehalten werden. **024** Präsentationsmodell IAA Frankfurt, Wettbewerb 1998. Die innenräumlichen Qualitäten wurden anhand maßstäblicher Modelle [1:87] überprüft.

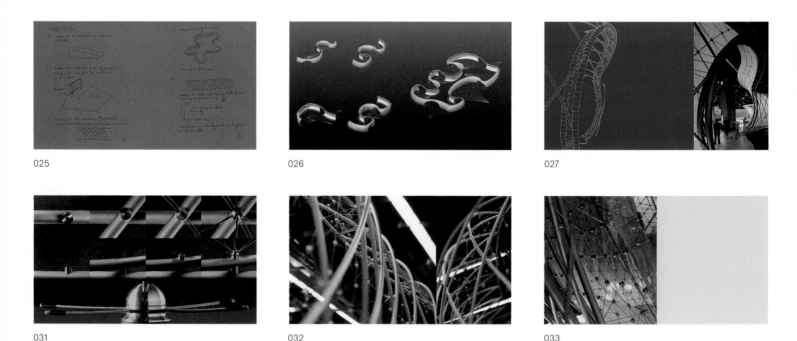

025

026

027

031

032

033

025 Werner Sobek, design sketches for the 1998 competition. The structure of the 'loop' consists of a small number of components permitting assembly in self-contained work units. 026 3D models of the exhibition stands with radiuses of construction. Left: TMS Tokyo Motor Show 1999 [upper left], NAIAS Detroit 2000/2001 [upper right], Geneva Motor Show 2000/2001 [lower left], Paris Motor Show 2000 [lower right]. Right: IAA Frankfurt 1999. The complex shapes of the floor plan of the exhibition stands were generated from only three radiuses [both as inner and outer radius]. 027 Left: Archway during workshop planning. Right: Completed archway at the IAA Frankfurt 1999. The coordination of the various CAD systems that provided the data for the workshop plans was a special achievement. 028 Positional plan of the rope mesh, IAA Frankfurt 1999. The primary structure of stainless steel pipes was adjusted to the regular geometry. The definition of the geometry was carried out on the basis of a "geometrical formation". The geometry of the stainless steel mesh was established as a secondary structure in dependence on the prescribed primary geometry through an analytical determination of form. This resulted in a mesh model as basis for the manufacture of the rope mesh and for cutting the panes of glass. 029 Left: Exploded isometric drawing of the structural planes, IAA Frankfurt 1999. Right: Detail of 'loop'. 030 Left: Detail of rod and rope mesh junctions. A total of 472 diagonally running rods curved along two axes formed the skeleton of the 'loop'. The structure had a height of 5.60 m and a total length of 306 m at its vertical mid-point. The supporting rods were inserted into torus-shaped foundations and were interconnected by means of a total of 1,600 rod junctions. The structure supported a mesh consisting of stainless steel rope with a total length of approx. 6,300 m that was tied to the skeleton by means of approx. 1,800 m of anchoring rope. The mesh supported the glass shell: approx. 12,000 triangular panes of glass with an edge length of 50—60 cm, held in place by 5,840 rope mesh junctions [IAA Frankfurt 1999]. Right: Exploded view of a 3D model of the rope mesh junction. Through the connection of two ropes, the junction creates the rhombic geometry of the rope mesh. The junction is held in place at the joints of the primary supporting frame-work by means of adjustable anchoring ropes. Various turned stainless steel and pressed EPDM parts in rotationally symmetrical arrangement serve the various functions of the complex component part: the upper clamping plate, the upper supporting disk, the star-shaped spacer and the lower supporting disk hold the panes of glass on the supporting saddle through form closure and clamping. On this saddle, the mesh ropes are joined through squeezing by means of a clamping plate. The screwed on spherical dome allows for the connection of the anchoring ropes in all required azimuth and zenithal angles. 031 Rod and rope mesh junctions—assembly sequence. 032 'Loop' structure with rope mesh, IAA Frankfurt 1999. The course of planning revealed that, due to its complex geometry, the primary structure could not be obtained from rods curved only along one axis. As a consequence, planners had to fall back on a more demanding bending technique. 033 Trial assembly in the Augustin hall in Ingolstadt. In Mai 1999, a 20-meter section of the 'loop' was erected, allowing for the first testing of the light and film projections in exhibition conditions. 034 Various design details with lettering. At the interface between graphic and linguistic communication, typography is of special significance. 035 Left: Detail of 'loop'. Right: Detail of communication walls at the Geneva Motor Show 2000. The formal characteristic of 'transparence' was rendered in the lettering. Large format letterings were omitted in the satin frosting of the glass. 036 Detail of communication walls at the Geneva Motor Show 2000. "For me, design is also philosophy. Paul Renner, Bodoni, Frutiger or Otl Aicher have given expression to their view of the world and hence also to their time." [Michael Keller]

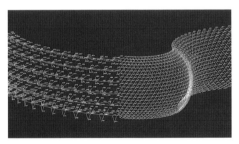

028

029

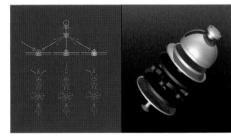

030

034

035

036

025 Werner Sobek, Entwurfsskizzen Wettbewerb 1998. Die Konstruktion des ›Loop‹ besteht aus wenigen Komponenten, die den Aufbau in geschlossenen Arbeitsschritten erlauben. **026** 3-D-Modelle der Messestände mit Konstruktionsradien. Links: TMS Tokyo Motor Show 1999 [o. l.], NAIAS Detroit 2000/2001 [o. r.], Internationaler Automobilsalon Genf 2000/2001 [u. l.], Mondial de l'Automobile Paris 2000 [u. r.]. Rechts: IAA Frankfurt 1999. Die komplexen Grundrissformen der Messestände wurden aus nur drei Radien [jeweils als Innen- und Außenradius] generiert. **027** Links: Torbogen, Werkstattplanung. Rechts: Realisierter Tordurchgang, IAA Frankfurt 1999. Eine besondere Leistung war die Koordination verschiedener CAD-Systeme, die die Daten für die Werkstattplanungen lieferten. **028** Positionsplan Seilnetz, IAA Frankfurt 1999. Die Primärstruktur aus Edelstahlrohren wurde auf die Regelgeometrie abgestimmt. Die Definition erfolgte auf Basis einer geometrischen Formsetzung. Die Netzgeometrie des Edelstahlnetzes wurde als Sekundärkonstruktion abhängig von der vorgegebenen Primärgeometrie durch analytische Formfindung ermittelt. Daraus ergab sich ein Maschenmodell als Grundlage für die Konfektion des Seilnetzes und für den Scheibenzuschnitt. **029** Links: Explosionsisometrie der Konstruktionsebenen, IAA Frankfurt 1999. Rechts: ›Loop‹, Detail. **030** Links: Stab- und Seilnetzknoten, Detail. Insgesamt 472 diagonal verlaufende, zweiachsig gekrümmte Stäbe bildeten das Skelett des ›Loop‹. Die Abwicklungslänge betrug in Äquatorhöhe 306 m bei einer Gesamtkonstruktionshöhe von 5,60 m. Die Tragstäbe waren in torusförmige Fundamente eingesteckt und wurden durch 1 600 Stabknoten miteinander verbunden. In die Konstruktion eingehängt und über Abspannseile [ca. 1 800 m] rückverspannt waren ca. 6 300 m Edelstahl-Seilnetze. Diese trugen die gläserne Hülle: ca. 12 000 dreieckige Glasscheiben mit einer Kantenlänge von 50–60 cm, gehalten von 5 840 Seilnetzknoten [IAA Frankfurt 1999]. Rechts: 3-D-Modell des Seilnetzknotens, Explosionszeichnung. Der Knoten erzeugt durch die Verbindung von je zwei Seilen die Rautengeometrie des Seilnetzes. Er ist durch justierbare Abspannseile an den Fügepunkten des Primärtragwerks gehalten. Edelstahldreh- und EPDM-Stanzteile in rotationssymmetrischer Anordnung dienen den verschiedenen Funktionen des komplexen Bauteils: Der obere Klemmteller, die obere Auflagerscheibe, der Distanzstern und die untere Auflagerscheibe halten die Glasscheiben durch Formschluss und Klemmung auf dem Auflagersattel. Auf diesem werden die Netzseile mit einem Klemmteller durch Pressung verbunden. Der aufgeschraubte Kugeldom erlaubt den Anschluss der Abspannseile in allen erforderlichen azimuthalen und zenitalen Winkeln. **031** Stab- und Seilnetzknoten, Montagefolge. **032** ›Loop‹-Konstruktion mit Seilnetz, IAA Frankfurt 1999. Im Verlauf der Planung zeigte sich, dass die Primärstruktur aufgrund ihrer komplexen Geometrie nicht aus einachsig gekrümmten Stäben erzeugt werden konnte. Dies hatte zur Folge, dass auf eine anspruchsvollere Biegetechnik zurückgegriffen werden musste. **033** Probeaufbau, Augustinhalle Ingolstadt. Im Mai 1999 wurde ein 20 Meter langer Abschnitt des ›Loop‹ originalgetreu aufgebaut. Hier konnten erstmals die Licht- und Filmprojektionen unter Messebedingungen getestet werden. **034** Verschiedene Gestaltungsdetails mit Schriftzügen. Als Schnittstelle zwischen graphischer und sprachlicher Kommunikation kommt der Typographie besondere Bedeutung zu. **035** Links: ›Loop‹, Detail. Rechts: Kommunikationswände, Detail, Internationaler Automobilsalon Genf 2000. Das formale Merkmal der Transparenz wurde auf die Schrift übertragen. Großformatige Schriftzüge wurden bei der Satinierung des Glases ausgespart. **036** Kommunikationswände, Detail, Internationaler Automobilsalon Genf 2000. »Für mich ist Gestaltung immer auch Philosophie. Paul Renner, Bodoni, Frutiger oder Otl Aicher haben ihre Weltanschauung und damit auch ihre Zeit zum Ausdruck gebracht.« [Michael Keller]

037

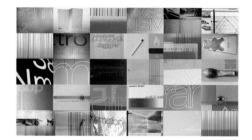

038

039

043

044

045

037 Clothes of the exhibition stand personnel, IAA Frankfurt 1999. A special collection of clothes was designed for the personnel, which enhanced the impression of lightness and transparency. Under the direction of KMS, a clothing manufacturer prepared the patterns and manufactured, in accordance with the chosen materials and colors, the required quantities. **038** Details of the design and furnishings, IAA Frankfurt 1999. **039** Detailed views of communication walls. The outline type was chosen as the typographical rendering of the transparency motif. The basis was always the Audi trade show font Audi Sans Extended in bold and regular. **040 and 041** Transparent complimentary bags, details and trade show impressions. The guideline was to design the bags out of transparent or translucent material in analogy with the appearance of the exhibition stand as a whole. Only few manufacturers were able to process transparent synthetic material in sufficient thickness. Only through intensive research was it possible to secure production. The effort proved worthwhile: due to their material and coloring, the bags gave the effect of countless 'loop' particles, like miniaturized Audi exhibition stands, as it were. **042** Left: Color design. The dominant color of the stand was orange. It signals energy and warmth and added a lively note to the very technologically oriented site. Moreover, this color picked up the thread from previous exhibitions and thus became a distinguishing mark recognizable worldwide. Right: Materials. All of the materials used were coordinated in terms of the color design. **043** Materials. The limitation to a small number of carefully processed materials of high quality was part of the consistent implementation of the master plan and also reflected Audi's claim to its position as a manufacturer of high-end automobiles. The surface treatments were chosen to suit the materials used, enhancing the character of the stainless steel, glass and wood. Aside from the so-called natural materials, products with specific properties especially developed for the exhibition were processed as well such as the extremely durable polyamide fiber carpet developed in cooperation with the architects. **044** Left: Detail of shadow and projection onto the 'loop'. Right: Boxes containing the triangular glass panes for the 'loop', IAA Frankfurt 1999. In a complex process such as the building of an exhibition installation, conventional design tasks constitute but a fraction of the activity. In this context, the task of architecture and design could be defined as 'designing through coordination'. It is always a matter of deriving and defining the guidelines from the master plan and—later in the cooperation—of reacting adequately to concrete limitations and unforeseeable events. The process is evolutionary, design and architecture being frequently a case of selection. We choose between alternatives, we correct developments and reject solutions that depart from the master plan. Meticulous quality control is also an important part of the work. Through a process of steering and filtering, we step by step approach a result that agrees with the basic idea of the master plan. **045** Glass with a degree of satin-frosting of 1/1—scanning electron photograph. In numerous experiments, printed, etched and satin-frosted glass was tested with regard to its suitability for displaying projections. Eventually, a degree of satin-frosting [1/1] was found that satisfied all of the requirements. Every component of the projection of light, images and film was then adjusted to this glass.

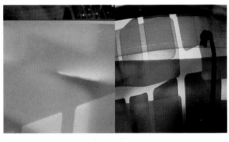

040

041

042

046

047

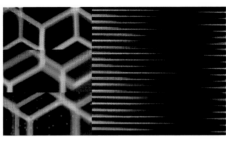

048

037 Kleidung Standpersonal, IAA Frankfurt 1999. Für die Einkleidung des Personals wurde eine Kollektion entworfen, die den Eindruck des Leichten und Transparenten verstärkte. Unter Anleitung von KMS erstellte eine Konfektionsfirma die Schnitte und fertigte entsprechend der getroffenen Material- und Farbauswahl die geforderten Stückzahlen. **038** Details des Designs und der Ausstattung, IAA Frankfurt 1999. **039** Kommunikationswände, Detailansichten. Als typographische Umsetzung des Transparenz-Gedankens wurde die Outline-Type gewählt. Grundlage war stets die Audi-Hausschrift Audi Sans Extended in den Schnitten Bold und Regular. **040 und 041** Transparente Tragetaschen, Details und Messeimpressionen. Die Vorgabe lautete, die Taschen analog zur Gesamtanmutung des Standes aus einem transparenten oder transluzenten Material zu gestalten. Nur wenige Produzenten waren in der Lage, transparenten Kunststoff in ausreichender Stärke zu verarbeiten. Nur durch intensive Recherchen konnte die Produktion gesichert werden. Der Aufwand lohnte sich: Durch Material und Farbgebung wirkten die Tragetaschen wie zahllose ›Loop‹-Partikel, gewissermaßen wie Audi-Stände im Kleinen. **042** Links: Farbkonzept. Orange war die bestimmende Farbe des Standes. Sie signalisiert Energie und Wärme und gab der stark ausgeprägten technischen Anmutung eine lebendige Note. Darüber hinaus knüpfte der Farbton an die vorangegangenen Messeauftritte an und wurde so zum weltweit wiedererkennbaren Merkmal. Rechts: Materialien. Alle verwendeten Materialien wurden auf der Basis des Farbkonzeptes aufeinander abgestimmt. **043** Materialien. Die Reduzierung auf wenige hochwertige und sorgfältig verarbeitete Materialien gehörte zur konsequenten Umsetzung des Gesamtkonzepts und spiegelte auch den Anspruch von Audi als Automobilhersteller im Premiumsegment wider. Die Oberflächenbehandlungen waren materialgerecht und unterstützten den Charakter der verwendeten Materialien, im Wesentlichen Edelstahl, Glas und Holz. Neben den sog. natürlichen Materialien wurden für den Messeauftritt entwickelte Produkte mit spezifischen Eigenschaften verarbeitet, so etwa der zusammen mit den Architekten entwickelte, extrem strapazierfähige Teppichboden aus Polyamidfasergewebe. **044** Links: Schatten und Projektion auf den ›Loop‹, Detail. Rechts: Kisten mit den dreieckigen Glasscheiben für den ›Loop‹, IAA Frankfurt 1999. In einem komplexen Vorgang wie dem Entstehen einer Messeinstallation stellen die gestalterischen Tätigkeiten nur einen Bruchteil des Handelns dar. »Durch Koordination gestalten« – so könnte die Aufgabe von Architektur und Design hier definiert werden. Immer geht es darum, die Vorgaben aus dem Konzept abzuleiten, zu definieren und später in der Zusammenarbeit auf konkret auftretende Einschränkungen, Hindernisse und Unvorhersehbarkeiten adäquat zu reagieren. Der Prozess ist evolutionär, Design und Architektur sind oft eine Art Selektionsinstanz. Wir wählen zwischen Alternativen aus, korrigieren Entwicklungen, verwerfen Lösungen, die sich vom Konzept entfernen. Die akribische Qualitätskontrolle ist ein wichtiger Bestandteil der Arbeit. Indem wir steuern und filtern, nähern wir uns schrittweise einem Ergebnis, das mit dem konzeptionellen Grundgedanken übereinstimmt. **045** Glas mit Satinierungsgrad 1/1, Rasterelektonenaufnahme. In zahlreichen Versuchen wurden bedruckte, geätzte und satinierte Gläser hinsichtlich ihrer Projektionsfähigkeit getestet. Schließlich wurde ein Satinierungsgrad [1/1] gefunden, der allen gewünschten Anforderungen gerecht wurde. Auf dieses Glas wurden alle Komponenten der Licht-, Bild- und Filmprojektion abgestimmt.

049

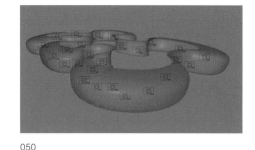

050

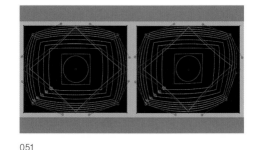

051

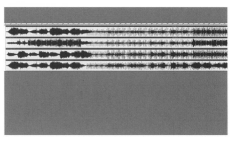

055

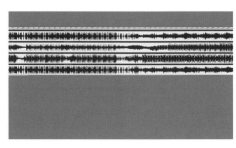

056

057

046 to 049 Film projection onto the 'loop'—stills, IAA Frankfurt 1999. Primarily, continually changing sequences of abstract structures were displayed. A second, corresponding grid was thus superimposed over the mesh provided by the architecture. The tones of color and the motifs varied from one bay of the 'loop' to another. Thus, for example, the presentation of the A2 was characterized by the theme of "lightness": the predominant color tone was turquoise, and the projection showed rising bubbles of air and water. References to features of the vehicles were established through an intermittent projection of individual words. In regular intervals, a synchronically projected common sequence could be seen in all of the bays, which bathed the entire 'loop' in a yellow-orange light. **050** Representation of the projector positions, IAA Frankfurt 1999. In order to achieve optimal results in the projection of moving images onto the 'loop' surface curved along two axes, 25 video projectors of the latest generation as well as extensive hardware and software in audio and video technology customized to suit the requirements of the 'loop' were used at the IAA in Frankfurt. **051** Gradual distortion scheme. Already during the production of the film, the shots were "distorted" in such a way that flawless images resulted from the projection onto the double curved 'loop' surface. It was necessary to grind the lenses of the projectors in various ways, since the surfaces varied from concave to convex. **052** Illumination and projection, section of the system, IAA Frankfurt 1999. The upper and lower edges of the 'loop' were fitted with a continuous strip of light that matched the film projections in terms of color. For this purpose, 137 background lights with a color mixing system were set up [specially manufactured floodlights with RGB fluorescent tubes]. Individually dimmable fluorescent lamps equipped with filters were used as lighting devices. The light-emitting openings were covered with opal glass. For the purpose of accentuating the middle and upper areas by means of color, 88 spotlights with swiveling heads were used. The 'loop' was additionally illuminated from behind. **053** Symbolic plan of the light fixtures used at the IAA Frankfurt 1999. All in all, 1,600 kW of electricity were required, and 650 daylight, multistage and profile spotlights were installed in the ceiling. **054** Detail of the 'loop' illumination and section of a monitor with media control program. **055 to 058** Oscillogram of the soundtrack. Five different nine-minute musical pieces were associated with the five vehicle exhibition areas. These pieces were playing in parallel and were divided into segments that could be put together in varying order. The compositions were coordinated in such a way that is was possible to superimpose all of the segments such that the individual zones were also perceived acoustically as continuous and yet differentiated sub-worlds. The individual sound sequences could be synchronized with various image sequences. This resulted in a twelve-hour presentation without repetitions of identical image-sound combinations. **059** Rear façade of the exhibition hall in Geneva, February 2000 [long exposure]. **060** Left: Bending process for 'loop' pipes—workshop. Right: pre-fabricated splines, IAA Frankfurt 1999. The bending process for the 'loop' pipes was based on the 3D spline data and allowed for a maximal approximation of the shape of the pipes to the theoretical guideline. For about five minutes, the 35 kg pipe passed through the rolls, was thereby bent with a varying radius and manually twisted, by means of a custom-made device, about the rod axis. The geometry of the rod was verified by means of a caliber adjustable along three axes. Subsequently, the holes were drilled at the junction points, since drilling before bending would have led to cracks and deformations in the holes. Finally, the rods were marked for later assembly in sections.

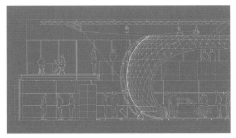

052

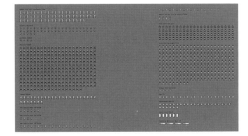

053

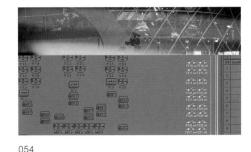

054

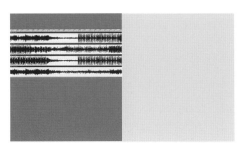

058

059

060

046 bis 049 Filmprojektion auf den ›Loop‹, Standbilder, IAA Frankfurt 1999. Überwiegend wurden Sequenzen mit abstrakten Strukturen gezeigt, die sich fortwährend veränderten. Dadurch legte sich über das von der Architektur vorgegebene Netz ein zweites, ihm entsprechendes Raster. Farbstimmung und Motive waren in den verschiedenen Buchten des ›Loop‹ unterschiedlich. So bestimmte z. B. das Thema »Leichtigkeit« die Präsentation des A2: der vorherrschende Farbton war türkisblau, die Projektion zeigte aufsteigende Luft- und Wasserblasen. Durch intermittente Projektion einzelner Begriffe wurden Bezüge zu den Eigenschaften der Fahrzeuge hergestellt; in regelmäßigen Abständen war in allen Buchten eine synchron projizierte gemeinsame Sequenz zu sehen, die den gesamten ›Loop‹ in ein gelb-oranges Licht tauchte. **050** Darstellung der Beamerpositionen, IAA Frankfurt 1999. Um ein optimales Ergebnis bei der Projektion bewegter Bilder auf die zweiachsig gekrümmte ›Loop‹-Oberfläche zu erzielen, wurden auf der IAA in Frankfurt u. a. 25 Videobeamer der neuesten Generation und eine umfangreiche, speziell auf die Anforderungen des ›Loop‹ abgestimmte Hard- und Software der Audio- und Videotechnik eingesetzt. **051** Graduelles Verzerrungsschema. Bereits bei der Filmproduktion wurden die Aufnahmen so »verzerrt«, dass bei der Projektion auf die zweifach gekrümmte Loopoberfläche fehlerfreie Bilder entstanden. Die Linsen der Projektoren mussten unterschiedlich geschliffen werden, da die Flächen von konkav bis konvex wechselten. **052** Beleuchtung und Projektion, Systemschnitt, IAA Frankfurt 1999. Der ›Loop‹ wurde am oberen und unteren Rand mit einem durchgängigen Lichtband versehen, das farblich auf die Projektionen abgestimmt war. Hierzu wurden 137 Hintergrundleuchten mit Farbmischsystem positioniert [Sonderanfertigung mit RGB-Neonröhren]. Als Leuchtmittel wurden befilterte, einzeln dimmbare Leuchtstofflampen verwendet, die Lichtaustrittsöffnungen mit Opalglas abgedeckt. Zur farbigen Akzentuierung des mittleren und oberen Bereiches wurden 88 kopfbewegte Scheinwerfer eingesetzt. Der ›Loop‹ wurde zusätzlich von hinten angestrahlt. **053** Symbolplan der eingesetzten Leuchten, IAA Frankfurt 1999. Insgesamt wurden 1600 kW Strom benötigt und 650 Tageslicht-, Stufen- und Profilscheinwerfer in die Decke gehängt. **054** Detail der ›Loop‹-Beleuchtung und Ausschnitt eines Monitors mit Mediensteuerungsprogramm. **055 bis 058** Klangoszillogramm des Soundtracks. Den fünf Fahrzeugbereichen waren fünf unterschiedliche, jeweils neun Minuten lange Musikstücke zugeordnet, die parallel zueinander erklangen und in Segmente unterteilt waren, die in unterschiedlicher Reihenfolge zusammengesetzt werden konnten. Die Kompositionen waren so aufeinander abgestimmt, dass alle Segmente überlagert werden konnten, so dass die einzelnen Zonen auch akustisch als zusammenhängende, jedoch differenzierte Subwelten wahrgenommen wurden. Die einzelnen Klangsequenzen waren mit verschiedenen Bildfolgen synchronisierbar. Daraus entstand eine zwölfstündige Inszenierung ohne Wiederholungen identischer Bild-Ton-Kombinationen. **059** Rückfassade der Messehalle in Genf, Februar 2000 [Langzeitbelichtung]. **060** Links: Biegeverfahren ›Loop‹-Rohre, Werkstatt. Rechts: Vorkonfektionierte Splines, IAA Frankfurt 1999. Das Biegeverfahren der ›Loop‹-Rohre basierte auf den 3-D-Splinedaten und erlaubte eine maximale Annäherung der Rohrform an die theoretische Vorgabe. In ungefähr fünf Minuten lief das 35 kg schwere Rohr durch die Walzen, wurde dabei mit wechselndem Radius gebogen und manuell durch eine selbst gebaute Vorrichtung um die Stabachse verdreht. Anhand einer in drei Achsen einstellbaren Lehre wurde die Stabgeometrie überprüft. Danach wurden an den Kreuzungspunkten die Bohrungen hergestellt, da ein Bohren vor dem Biegen zu Rissen und Verformungen der Löcher geführt hätte. Abschließend wurden die Stäbe für die spätere feldweise Montage gekennzeichnet.

061

062

063

067

068

069

061 Connectors and spacers for 'loop' pipes. Running on two levels, the stainless steel pipes of the 'loop' were joined at their 1,592 points of intersection [IAA Frankfurt 1999] in such a way as to prevent shifting and bending. **062** Set-up and assembly, IAA Frankfurt 1999. The first step in the assembly of the 'loop' was the erection of the primary supporting structure. It consisted of three-dimensionally bent, diagonally positioned stainless steel pipes [Ø 48,3 mm, wall thickness 4mm]. These ran on two levels and were connected at their points of intersection by means of clamps to prevent shifting. This completed and stabilized the primary structure. At the bottom, they were clamped into a foundational structure made of steel sections, while at the top, they were held in place by an upper edge pipe. For further stabilization of this skeleton, the points of intersection were connected horizontally through stainless steel tensioning ropes. Subsequently, clamp junctions and anchoring ropes were attached to the intersections of the pipes. A net with a 40-centimeter diamond-shaped mesh made of three-millimeter stainless steel ropes was stretched at a small distance in front of the primary structure and fastened to the clamp junctions. **063** Assembly of the panes of glass, IAA Frankfurt 1999. Structural EPDM parts are mounted on the junction points for receiving the triangular panes of safety glass. The panes of glass were inserted at their corner points, aligned and finally secured permanently by means of a clamping plate. Every clamping junction holds six panes of glass and has a diameter of only five centimeters. About 12,000 glass triangles in 3,000 different sizes were required for the surface of 1,800 square meters. **064** Point of intersection with mounted panes of glass, IAA Frankfurt 1999. In accordance with the positional plans of workshop planning, all of the panes of glass were individually numbered and securely packed by sections in shipping crates. **065 to 067** Impressions of the assembly work, IAA Frankfurt 1999. In spite of its size and complex structure, the 'loop' was set up within a span of nine days [IAA Frankfurt 1999]. This relatively short assembly time was made possible by finely tuned logistics and detail planning. The structure consisted of a small number of components that could be joined in stages, thus permitting assembly in self-contained work units. Construction took place around the clock in a three-shift operation. **068** Preparation of the vehicles, IAA Frankfurt 1999 **069** Barriers at the exhibition stand just prior to opening, Geneva Motor Show 2000. **070** Exhibition stand of AUDI AG, IAA Frankfurt 1999. September 12, 1999, just hours before the official opening of the International Auto Show. **071** Outside view of the 'loop', IAA Frankfurt 1999. "As free as the 'loop' may appear, it is not an arbitrary form, which somehow has been made to stand upright. The flowing three-dimensionality is 100 percent classical engineering and not something merely dreamt up by means of a computer and then constructed from papier mâché. We are dealing a lot with engineers all over the world. They are not only familiar with Audi, but they also know the slogan 'advancement through technology'—even in German." [Christoph Ingenhoven] **072** Customer center and visitors' lounge, view of the 'loop' from inside, IAA Frankfurt 1999.

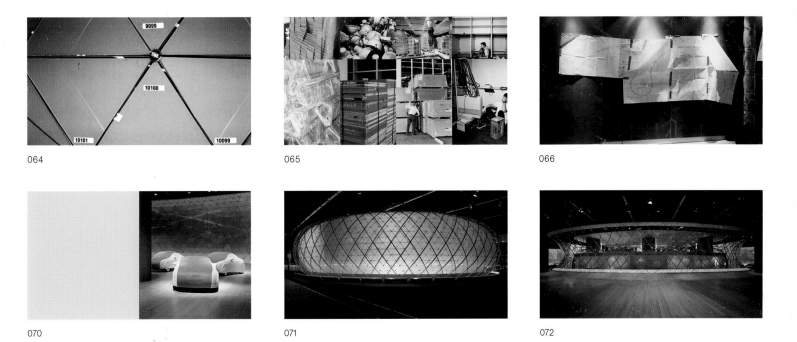

064 065 066

070 071 072

061 Verbindungs- und Distanzstücke der ›Loop‹-Rohre. Die in zwei Ebenen verlaufenden Edelstahlrohre des ›Loop‹ wurden in den 1592 Kreuzungspunkten [IAA Frankfurt 1999] unverschieblich und biegesteif miteinander verbunden. **062** Aufbau- und Montage, IAA Frankfurt 1999. Der erste Schritt bei der Montage der ›Loop‹-Konstruktion war die Aufstellung der primären Tragstruktur. Sie bestand aus räumlich gebogenen, diagonal gestellten Edelstahlrohren [ø 48,3 mm, Wandstärke 4mm]. Diese verliefen in zwei Ebenen und wurden in ihrem Kreuzungspunkt durch eine Klemme unverschieblich miteinander verbunden. Damit war die Primärkonstruktion geschlossen und stabilisiert. Im Fußpunkt waren sie in einer Fundamentkonstruktion aus Stahlprofilen eingespannt und am Kopfpunkt durch ein oberes Randrohr gehalten. Zur weiteren Stabilisierung dieses Skeletts wurden die Kreuzungspunkte durch horizontal verlaufende Edelstahlspannseile verbunden. Anschließend wurden an den Rohrkreuzungen Klemmknoten und Abspannseile befestigt. Daran war ein Seilnetz mit rund 40 cm großen, rautenförmigen Maschen aus drei Millimeter starken Edelstahlseilen in geringem Abstand vor die Primärkonstruktion gespannt. **063** Montage der Glasscheiben, IAA Frankfurt 1999. Auf den Knotenpunkten sitzen EPDM-Formteile zur Aufnahme der Scheiben aus Sicherheitsglas. Die Gläser wurden an ihren Spitzen eingeklipst, ausgerichtet und abschließend durch einen Klemmteller dauerhaft gesichert. Jeder Klemmknoten fasst sechs Scheiben und hat einen Durchmesser von nur fünf Zentimetern. Für die 1800 qm große Fläche waren ca. 12 000 Glasdreiecke in 3 000 unterschiedlichen Formaten erforderlich. **064** Knotenpunkt mit montierten Glasscheiben, IAA Frankfurt 1999. Alle Glasscheiben waren, entsprechend den Positionsplänen der Werkstattplanung, segmentweise und bruchsicher in Transportkisten verpackt und durchnummeriert. **065 bis 067** Impressionen vom Aufbau, IAA Frankfurt 1999. Der ›Loop‹ wurde trotz seiner Größe und komplexen Struktur innerhalb von neun Tagen aufgebaut [IAA Frankfurt 1999]. Ermöglicht wurde diese relativ kurze Montagezeit durch ausgefeilte Logistik und Detailplanung. Der Aufbau erfolgte im Drei-Schichten-Betrieb rund um die Uhr. **068** Vorbereitung der Fahrzeuge, IAA Frankfurt 1999. **069** Absperrungen am Stand kurz vor der Eröffnung, Internationaler Automobilsalon Genf 2000. **070** Messestand der AUDI AG, IAA Frankfurt 1999. 12. September 1999, wenige Stunden vor der offiziellen Eröffnung der Internationalen Automobil-Ausstellung. **071** Außenansicht ›Loop‹, IAA Frankfurt 1999. »So frei der ›Loop‹ auch aussieht, es ist keine willkürliche Form, die man irgendwie zum Stehen gebracht hat. Die fließende Dreidimensionalität ist zu 100 Prozent klassische Ingenieursarbeit und nicht nur mit dem Computer herbeigewünscht und am Ende aus Pappmaché gebaut. Wir haben viel mit Ingenieuren in aller Welt zu tun. Die kennen nicht nur Audi, sondern auch den Slogan Vorsprung durch Technik – sogar auf Deutsch.« [Christoph Ingenhoven] **072** Kundenzentrum und Besucherlounge, ›Loop‹-Ansicht von innen, IAA Frankfurt 1999.

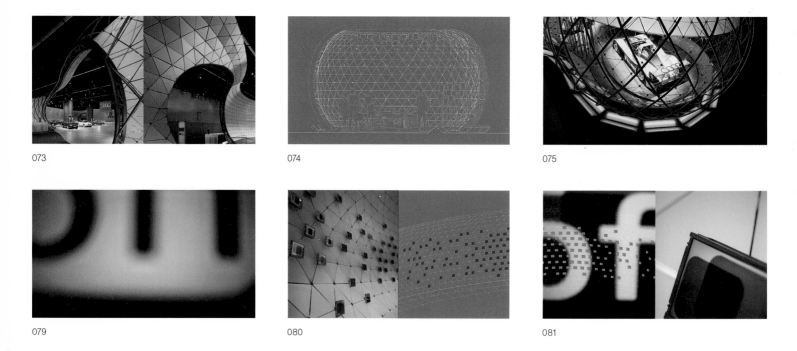

073

074

075

079

080

081

073 Main entrances, IAA Frankfurt 1999. The main access to the exhibition stand led through large gateways in the central axis of the stand. In front of the gateways there were information and brochure counters. **074** View of the highlight presentation of the R8, TMS Tokyo Motor Show 1999. **075** Highlight presentation of the R8, TMS Tokyo Motor Show 1999. The satin-frosted und transparent glass panes of the 'loop' were installed by sections into the structure in such a way that it was possible to see the vehicles and exhibits from all sides. In Tokyo, the 'loop' was shaped into a cocoon opened on one side. In this manner, the R8 was presented as the highlight of the exhibition as if contained in a giant display case. **076** Detail of a glass surface on vehicle communication, Geneva Motor Show 2000. The characteristic feature of "transparency" gained aesthetic autonomy and connected the various stands of the exhibition cycle in the manner of corporate design. **077** Monitor forest for the highlight presentation of the A2, IAA Frankfurt 1999. The respective exhibition highlight was presented by an installation of monitors, rather than by a traditional automobile advertising film. A "forest" of 27 staggered screens mounted at various heights showed synchronically running films. The dramatization was directed at the overall visual impression, which was obtained through sequences that were partly parallel, partly staggered and partly forming a large composite image. **078** Left: Film projection onto the 'loop' – still. Right: Highlight presentation of the A2 with monitor forest, IAA Frankfurt 1999. **079** Detail of monitor forest, IAA Frankfurt 1999. Apart from functional considerations, the idea behind this 'experimental' video installation was to exploit technological possibilities and thereby also help set the direction of future developments in communications design. **080** Monitor net and positional plan for the monitor net [right], Geneva Motor Show 2000. In Geneva, the concept of the monitor forest was rendered as a monitor net. Approx. 200 screens were attached directly to the rope mesh junctions of the 'loop' and were controlled in groups of 6. **081** Positional plan and details of the monitor net, Geneva Motor Show 2000. **082** Light and film projection, IAA Frankfurt 1999. **083** Light and film projection, TMS Tokyo Motor Show 1999. **084** Still of a projection sequence with animated outline typography, IAA Frankfurt 1999. Graphics or light? The overlapping of aesthetic, functional and semantic aspects of communication was an essential feature of the holistic design of the exhibition stand.

076

077

078

082

083

084

073 Hauptzugänge, IAA Frankfurt 1999. Der Hauptzugang in den Messestand erfolgte über großzügige Tordurchgänge in der Mittelachse des Standes. Vor den Durchgängen befanden sich die Informations- und Prospekttheken. **074** Ansicht Highlightpräsentation R8, TMS Tokyo Motor Show 1999. **075** Highlightpräsentation R8, TMS Tokyo Motor Show 1999. Die satinierten und transparenten Gläser des ›Loop‹ wurden feldweise so in die Konstruktion eingesetzt, dass die Fahrzeuge und Exponate von allen Seiten einsehbar waren. In Tokyo wurde der ›Loop‹ zu einem einseitig geöffneten Kokon geformt. Der R8 wurde so, wie in einer überdimensionalen Vitrine, als Messe-Highlight präsentiert. **076** Detail einer Glasfläche zur Fahrzeugkommunikation, Internationaler Automobilsalon Genf 2000. Das Merkmal »Transparenz« gewann ästhetische Autonomie und verband die verschiedenen Stände des Messezyklus in der Art eines Corporate Designs miteinander. **077** Monitorwald, Highlightpräsentation A2, IAA Frankfurt 1999. Statt eines herkömmlichen Fahrzeug-Werbefilms präsentierte eine Monitorinstallation das jeweilige Messe-Highlight. Ein »Monitorwald« aus 27 in unterschiedlicher Höhe montierten, räumlich versetzten Bildschirmen zeigte synchron ablaufende Filme. Die Dramaturgie war auf den visuellen Gesamteindruck gerichtet, der aus teils parallelen, teils zeitlich versetzten, teils zu einem Großbild sich ergänzenden Sequenzen gewonnen wurde. **078** Links: Filmprojektion auf den ›Loop‹, Standbild. Rechts: Highlightpräsentation A2 mit Monitorwald, IAA Frankfurt 1999. **079** Monitorwald, Detail, IAA Frankfurt 1999. Die Konzeption dieser experimentellen Video-Installationen folgte – neben den funktionalen Erwägungen – dem Anspruch, technische Möglichkeiten auszureizen und dadurch auch Weiterentwicklungen im Kommunikationsdesign mitzusteuern. **080** Monitornetz und Positionsplan für das Monitornetz [rechts], Internationaler Automobilsalon Genf 2000. In Genf wurde das Konzept des Monitorwaldes als Monitornetz umgesetzt. Hier waren ca. 200 Bildschirme direkt an den Seilnetzknoten des ›Loop‹ befestigt und wurden in Sechser-Gruppen einzeln angesteuert. **081** Positionsplan und Details Monitornetz, Internationaler Automobilsalon Genf 2000. **082** Licht- und Filmprojektion, IAA Frankfurt 1999. **083** Licht- und Filmprojektion, TMS Tokyo Motor Show 1999. **084** Standbild einer Projektionssequenz mit bewegter Outline-Typographie, IAA Frankfurt 1999. Graphik oder Licht? Die Überlagerung ästhetischer, funktionaler und inhaltlicher Aspekte der Kommunikation war ein wesentliches Merkmal der ganzheitlichen Gestaltung des Messestandes.

085

086

087

091

092

093

085 Left: Detail of the system of orientation, IAA Frankfurt 1999. Right: Clothes of exhibition stand personnel. The light installation of the system of orientation also contributed to the formal coherence of the master plan. 086 Left: Visitors' lounge, IAA Frankfurt 1999. Right: Furnishings of the lounge areas [Swan, Arne Jacobsen]. The freely accessible visitors' lounge was located on the upper floor—on the same level as the lounge of the board of directors. The lounge areas offered a comprehensive view onto the entire exhibition stand area. 087 and 088 Designer film Audi TT, monitor installation, IAA Frankfurt 1999. In a video documentary on the development of the form language of the Audi TT, five members of the design team offered insight into their work during a four-hour interview. To this end, the designers were asked to illustrate associatively various concepts. Transparencies were attached as drawing surfaces to frosted panes of glass. Five cameras simultaneously captured the events from the other side of the glass. At the IAA in Frankfurt, the synchronically running individual films were shown in an installation consisting of five portrait-format plasma screens. 089 Film for the motor gallery, IAA Frankfurt 1999. Motor, technology and safety exhibits were combined in a separate area. The atmosphere in this area contrasted with that of the so-called inner area of the 'loop'. Monitor installations displayed images of simulated motor combustion processes that were acoustically reinforced by the appropriate sound effects. 090 Motor scanner, motor gallery IAA Frankfurt 1999. By means of the motor scanner, visitors were able to obtain information about the exhibited vehicle engines. It was possible to target and optically activate the individual components of the engine block. The interior or the motor was made visible on a display screen according to the principle of an x-ray machine. Via a touch screen, visitors were able to call up the scanned components, while texts, animations and films explained their respective function. Following their use in the exhibitions, the motor scanners were integrated into the "museum mobile" that KMS designed for Audi in Ingolstadt. 091 and 092 Telematics installation, IAA Frankfurt 1999. An audiovisual installation consisting of three plasma monitors explained and visually demonstrated the communications and information functions of Audi's navigational system by means of a choreographic performance. 093 Impressions of the approach to the Geneva Motor Show 2000. 094 Final meeting with exhibition stand personnel, IAA Frankfurt 1999. "Now the crew receives training and an elaborate brochure, which contains not only all the details regarding work, but also tips for restaurants or dance clubs." [Michael Keller] 095 Left: The portfolio for visitors. The information was printed on pieces of card stock of the size of business cards, the backsides of which featured various illustrative motifs. All visitors received a plastic sleeve with a basic set and were able to add, depending on their personal interest, additional cards on topics such as "airbag", "safety" or "TDI" provided by exhibition stand personnel. Right: Brochure depot, IAA Frankfurt 1999. 096 Public attendance at the IAA Frankfurt 1999. "We started from the consideration that visitors normally spend hours, sometimes even days at a trade show. They don't see any daylight. It's a dreadful inner world, a black box. We wanted to counter this monotony with a structure." [Christoph Ingenhoven]

088

089

090

094

095

096

085 Links: Detail Orientierungssystem, IAA Frankfurt 1999. Rechts: Kleidung des Standpersonals. Auch die mediale Lichtinstallation des Orientierungssystems trug zur formalen Kohärenz des Gesamtkonzeptes bei. 086 Links: Besucher-Lounge, IAA Frankfurt 1999. Rechts: Möblierung der Loungebereiche [Schwan, Arne Jacobsen]. Die für alle Besucher frei zugängliche Lounge befand sich im Obergeschoss – auf gleicher Höhe wie die Vorstands-Lounge. Aus den Loungebereichen hatte man einen umfassenden Blick auf die gesamte Standfläche. 087 und 088 Designer-Film Audi TT, Bildschirm-Installation, IAA Frankfurt 1999. In einer Video-Dokumentation über die Entwicklung der Formensprache des Audi TT gaben fünf Mitglieder des Designer-Teams während eines insgesamt vier Stunden dauernden Interviews Einblick in ihre Arbeit. Dies geschah, indem sie aufgefordert wurden, verschiedene Begriffe assoziativ zu visualisieren. Hierzu wurden transparente Folien auf Milchglasscheiben befestigt. Fünf Kameras auf der anderen Seite der Scheiben fingen das Geschehen gleichzeitig ein. Auf der IAA in Frankfurt wurden die synchron laufenden Einzelfilme in einer Installation aus fünf hochformatigen Plasmabildschirmen gezeigt. 089 Film für die Motorengalerie, IAA Frankfurt 1999. Hier wurden Motoren-, Technik- und Sicherheitsexponate in einem eigenen Bereich zusammengefasst. Die Atmosphäre hob sich von derjenigen im sog. ›Innenbereich‹ des ›Loop‹ ab. Monitorinstallationen zeigten Aufnahmen, die den Verbrennungsprozess im Motor simulierten; akustisch wurden die Bilder durch entsprechende Geräuschcollagen untermalt. 090 Motorenscanner, Motorengalerie IAA Frankfurt 1999. Der Motorenscanner erlaubte es dem Besucher, sich über die ausgestellten Fahrzeugmotoren zu informieren. Die einzelnen Komponenten des Motorblocks konnten gezielt angesteuert und optisch aktiviert werden. Auf einem Bildschirm wurde das Innere des Motors nach dem Prinzip der Röntgenaufnahme sichtbar gemacht. Der Besucher konnte die durchleuchteten Komponenten via Touchscreen aufrufen; Texte, Animationen und Filme erläuterten ihre jeweilige Funktion. Nach dem Messe-Einsatz wurden die Motorenscanner in das von KMS für Audi konzipierte »museum mobile« in Ingolstadt integriert. 091 und 092 Telematic-Installation, IAA Frankfurt 1999. Eine Audio-/Videoinstallation aus drei Plasma-Monitoren erklärte und visualisierte die Kommunikations- und Informationsfunktionen des Audi-Navigationssystems durch eine choreographische Umsetzung. 093 Impressionen der Anfahrt zum Internationalen Automobilsalon Genf 2000. 094 Letzte Besprechung mit dem Standpersonal, IAA Frankfurt 1999. »Jetzt ist es so, dass die Crew Schulungen bekommt und eine aufwendig gestaltete Broschüre, in der nicht nur alles steht, was die Arbeit betrifft, sondern auch Tipps für Restaurants oder Diskotheken.« [Michael Keller] 095 Links: Das Besucherportfolio. Die Informationen waren auf visitenkartengroße Kartons gedruckt, auf deren Rückseiten verschiedene Bildmotive zu sehen waren. Jeder Besucher erhielt eine Plastikhülle mit einem Basis-Set und konnte nach eigenem Interesse weitere von Standbetreuern bereitgehaltene Karten zu Themen wie z. B. »Sicherheit«, »Audi Space Frame« oder »TDI« hinzufügen. Rechts: Broschüren-Depot, IAA Frankfurt 1999. 096 Besuchertage, IAA Frankfurt 1999. »Wir gingen von der Überlegung aus, dass die Besucher im Normalfall stunden-, manche auch tagelang auf der Messe sind. Sie sehen nichts vom Tageslicht, es ist eine furchtbare Innenwelt, eine Black Box. Gegen diese Eintönigkeit wollten wir eine Struktur setzen.« [Christoph Ingenhoven]

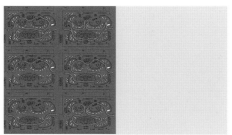

097

098

099

103

104

105

097 Diagrams of paths through the exhibition stand based on visitor movement analysis, IAA Frankfurt 1999. The goal was to offer visitors a high-quality exhibition stand, within which they could move comfortably. On the basis of visitor statistics of previous exhibitions, the ideal system of paths between groups of vehicles and exhibits was defined. **098** Visitors at the TMS Tokyo Motor Show 1999. **099** Highlight presentation of the A2, IAA Frankfurt 1999. **100 to 102** Impressions of the TMS Tokyo Motor Show 1999. **102** Left: Prince and Princess Mikasa [in the foreground]. On the occasion of the opening of the TMS Tokyo Motor Show, Japan's royal family also visited the exhibition stand of AUDI AG. For this purpose, a special route was kept open in the planning of the exhibition stand, on which the imperial car was able to traverse the stand. **103 and 104** Visitors' activities, Geneva Motor Show 2000. A satin-frosted pane of glass bore the inscription "Future is …", which visitors could complete with their own thoughts. Subsequently, a digital camera took a snapshot of the visitor alongside his or her personal 'definition of the future'. Visitors received one printout; another was included in the guest book—a wall, up to 60 m in length, the surface of which was completely covered with postcard size photographs by the end of the exhibition. **105 and 106** Children's drawings, Audi Kids Club, IAA Frankfurt 1999. Within eyeshot of the visitors' lounge at the IAA in Frankfurt was the "Audi Kids Club", where children were looked after within a pedagogical program that changed hourly. The furnishings were reduced to essentials in order to create as much room for free movement as possible. Transparent plastic cushions filled with hay served as seating. The tables were stacks of paper, on which the children could draw directly. The main attraction were large orange screens, on which children, using light pens, could draw their freely associated pictures on the theme of the future. The digitized works appeared simultaneously on the back wall of the bar in the visitors' lounge. **106** Right: Monitors at the staircase to the lounge areas, IAA Frankfurt 1999. **107 and 108** Impressions of the IAA Frankfurt 1999 and the Salon International de l'Automobile Geneva 2000.

100

101

102

106

107

108

097 Durchwegungsdiagramme der Personenstromanalyse, IAA Frankfurt 1999. Ziel war es, den Besuchern einen qualitativ hochwertigen Stand mit hohem Bewegungskomfort zu präsentieren. Auf der Grundlage von Besuchererhebungen vorangeganger Messen wurden die idealen Wegebeziehungen zwischen Fahrzeuggruppen und Ausstellungsexponaten definiert. **098** Besucher auf der TMS Tokyo Motor Show 1999. **099** Highlightpräsentation A2, IAA Frankfurt 1999. **100 bis 102** Impressionen TMS Tokyo Motor Show 1999. **102** Links: Prinz und Prinzessin Mikasa [im Vordergrund]. Zur Eröffnung der TMS Tokyo Motor Show besuchte die königliche Familie Japans auch den Messestand der AUDI AG. Zu diesem Zweck wurde bei der Standplanung eigens eine Trasse freigehalten, auf der der Kaiserwagen den Stand durchqueren konnte. **103 und 104** Besucheraktion, Internationaler Automobilsalon Genf 2000. Auf einer satinierten Glasscheibe war der Satzbeginn »Zukunft ist …« zu lesen, den die Besucher individuell ergänzen konnten. Anschließend wurde eine Digitalkamera ausgelöst, die sie/ihn neben der persönlichen Zukunftsdefinition fotografierte. Einen Ausdruck erhielten die Besucher, ein weiterer wurde in das Gästebuch aufgenommen – eine bis zu 60 m lange Wand, deren Fläche am Ende der Messe mit den postkartengroßen Fotos völlig bedeckt war. **105 und 106** Kinderzeichnungen, Audi Kids Club, IAA Frankfurt 1999. In Sichtweite der Besucher-Lounge befand sich auf der IAA in Frankfurt der »Audi Kids Club«. Hier wurden die Kinder bei stündlich wechselnden Programm pädagogisch betreut. Die Einrichtung war auf das Wesentliche reduziert, um möglichst großen Bewegungsfreiraum zu schaffen. Als Sitzgelegenheiten dienten heubefüllte Kissen aus transparentem Kunststoff, als Tische Papierstapel, auf denen die Kinder direkt malen konnten. Hauptattraktion waren orangefarbene Großbildschirme, auf welche die Kinder mit Leuchtstiften ihre Vorstellungen zum Thema Zukunft malen konnten. Die digitalisierten Bilder erschienen zeitgleich auf der Rückwand der Bar in der Besucher-Lounge. **106** Rechts: Monitore am Treppenaufgang zu den Loungebereichen, IAA Frankfurt 1999. **107 und 108** Impressionen IAA Frankfurt 1999 und Internationaler Automobilsalon Genf 2000.

Contract / **Commissioning Client: AUDI AG, Ingolstadt** Project: Exhibition Stands [IAA International Motor Show Frankfurt 1999, TMS Tokyo Motor Show 1999, NAIAS North American International Auto Show Detroit 2000, Geneva Motor Show 2000, Paris Motor Show 2000, NAIAS North American International Auto Show Detroit 2001, Geneva Motor Show 2001]

Concept / **Architecture: Ingenhoven Overdiek und Partner, Düsseldorf** Competition [Christoph Ingenhoven, Hinrich Schumacher, Ralf Dorsch-Rüter, Maximo Victoria, Sylvia Domke] Project Direction [Christoph Ingenhoven, Jürgen Overdiek, Michael Reiß] Design, Approval and Implementation Planning [Herwig Rott, Andreas Blum, Karan Djalaei, Holger Gravius, Liyang Guo, Manfred Junghans, Florian Nedden, Ingrid Sölken, Maximo Victoria, Christina Zippel] **Communications: KMS Team, Munich** Project Direction [Michael Keller, Christoph Rohrer, Thorsten Buch, Sabine Thernes] Project Management [Sven Sonnendorfer, Angelika Mosner, Ralph Ilsanker] Design [Sabine Klein, Simone Moll, Kolja Moormann, Uschi Pfingstgraf, Tina Schmerber, Stefanie Schröder, Carolin Weiß, Nerina Wilter] Text [Wolf Bruns, Dominik Neubauer] Production [Christina Baur, Karin Fugmann, Matthias Karpf, Angela Keesman, Bernd Müller, Christian Ring, Monika Weiglein]

Realization / **General Planning: Ingenhoven Overdiek Planungsgesellschaft GmbH & Co KG, Düsseldorf** Expense Budgeting, Scheduling, Tendering, Commissioning [Udo Rex, Andrea Thoma, Andreas Kramer] Site Management, Artistic Project Supervision [Udo Rex, Michael Reiß, Herwig Rott, Andrea Thoma] in cooperation with Severich & Partner GmbH & Co. KG, Roetgen [Karl-Heinz Severich, Rainer Glenk] **Supporting Framework Design** Werner Sobek Ingenieure GmbH, Stuttgart [Werner Sobek, Alfred Rein, Theodor Angelopoulos, Jörg Kuhn, Sandra Neaga, Ute Schenk, Klaus Straub, Arnold Walz, Ingo Weiss] **Lighting Design for Building** Werning Tropp Schmidt, Feldafing [Clemens Tropp, Ulrich Werning, Markus Tuppen] **Planning of Exhibition and Effect Lighting** FOUR TO ONE: scale design gmbH, Cologne [Michael Schmidt, Burkhard Jüterbock, Stephan Löper, Peter Rauscher, Elisabeth Jarych, Doreen Schlenner] **Lighting Engineering** Showtec, Cologne [Thomas Ickenroth, Sabine Huckenbeck, Heribert Dohm, Thomas Backhausen, Markus Boßdorf, Lars Wulff, Oliver Klaus, Ralf Berek, Frank Kähne, Volker Hardtke] Procon Multimedia AG, Glinde [Manfred Janßen, Carsten Will] **Architectural Acoustics** DS-Plan GmbH, Stuttgart **Visitor Movement Analysis** Durth Roos Consulting GmbH, Darmstadt [Thomas Weissenberger] **Fire Prevention** BPK Brandschutzplanung Klingsch, Düsseldorf [Wolfram Klingsch, Gürsel Dincer] **Architectural Models** Amalgam Modelmakers and Designers, Bristol, UK [Anthony Pallanca, Leo Saunders] Atelier Axel Oehlschlägel, Düsseldorf [Axel Oehlschlägel] Dörre Mobau GmbH, Düsseldorf [Reinhard Dörre] Lütke Modellbau, Olching [Manfred Lütke, Renate Kässbohrer] **Illustrations** Peter Wels, Hamburg **Model Photography** Studio Holger Knauf, Düsseldorf **Trade Fair Construction** Ambrosius Messebau, Frankfurt am Main [Joachim Hemberger, Jürgen Franz, Harald Heidrich, Denise Mindnich, Heinz Schlosser, Sven Berthold] George P. Johnson Company, Michigan, USA [Lynn Brockmann, Michael Cherubin, Chantelle Couchie, Anthony Motto, Colleen Zalmezak] A & A Expo International BV, Wijk bij Duurstede, NL [Anton Heidemann] **Steel Construction – 'Loop'** MBM Konstruktion GmbH, Möckmühl [Peter Müller, Georg Wieland, Jürgen Bauer, Michael Fritz] Seele, Gersthofen [Gerhard Seele, Emil Rohrer] **Steel Construction – Exhibition Stand** Klostermair Messebau Metalltechnik Logistik, Untermaxfeld [Klaus Klostermair, Klaus Kramer, Georg Birkmeir, Peter Schwarz] SYSCON GmbH, Hockenheim [Timo Burgmeier] **Steel Construction – 'Loop' and Exhibition Stand** E & C Engineering & Construction BV, Utrecht, NL [Wim Neven, Bram de Jonge] **Workshop Planning – 'Loop'** Alfa Plan GmbH Techniker & Ingenieure, Efringen-Kirchen [Armin Kainz, Waldemar Oswald, Klaus Volker Kniffka] **Glass Processing – 'Loop'** Andreas Oswald GmbH Metallbau/Konstruktiver Glasbau, Munich [Bernhard Homeier, Ernst Homeier] **Product Development of Carpet Floor** Carpet Concept Objekt-Teppichboden GmbH, Bielefeld [Thomas Trenkamp] **Graphical Realization** Schüttenberg GmbH, Düsseldorf [Felix Schüttenberg, Ernst-Dieter Schüttenberg, Ralf Nieß, Jürgen Tröger, Markus Scholz, Frank Honeiker, Reza Riahi, Renate Kraatz] Reger Studios, Munich [Peter Knödler, Thomas Maurer] **Technical Exhibits** Hüttinger Exhibition Engineering, Schwaig bei Nürnberg [Kurt Hüttinger, Armin Beck] **Show Cars and Technical Exhibits** Uedelhoven Studios, Gaimersheim **Clothing Collection for Exhibition Stand Personnel** Mey & Edlich GmbH & Co. KG, Munich [Henk Fleischmann, Birgit Henniger] **Movement Systems** BUMAT Bewegungssysteme GmbH, Hockenheim **General Equipment for Exhibition Stand Construction** Klostermair Messebau, Untermaxfeld [Klaus Klostermair, Klaus Kramer, Georg Birkmeier, Peter Appel, Peter Schwarz] **General Equipment for Lighting Engineering** Eschelbach Lichttechnik, Murnau am Staffelsee [Christian Eschelbach] **General Equipment for Interior** Herkommer + Gutbrod, Ingolstadt [Christian Leitmeier] **Sampling** Tischlerei Jagsch GmbH & Co. KG, Düsseldorf [Dieter Jagsch] Fries Innenausbau, Düsseldorf [Rainer Fries, Angelika Fries] **Film** velvet Mediendesign GmbH, Munich [Anne Böck, Arndt Buss-von Kuk, Luis Castrillo, Georgia Caramichu, Simone Haberland, Christian Künstler, Manfred Laumer, Claudius Schulz, Conny Unger, Matthias Zentner] **Music** TTM Production, Freising [Andreas List, Jürgen Lang, Jochen Seibert] **Design and Implementation of Audiovisual Media System** Michael Nicht + Partner, Schlichting [Michael Nicht, Michael Saddey, Peter Schneekloth] **Audiovisual Media Technology** A.D.A.M. Showtechnik GmbH, Willroth [Jürgen Starrmann, Wulf Issinger] Amptown Verleih GmbH & Co. KG, Hamburg [Christian Tesche, Ulf Sikora, Matthias Müllenbach] Gahrens + Battermann, Bergisch Gladbach [Bernd Nössler, Stefan Müller] Lang Audiovision AG, Lindlar; mediaMotion AG, Cologne [Ralf Stupp, Thomas Ahr] Neumann & Müller GmbH, Munich [Martin Schiller, Patrick Eckerlin] MEDIA!AG, Munich; PASS GmbH, Steinheim-Höpfingheim [Stefan Tulipan] Riemer GmbH Communication-Systems, Soest [Hans-Georg Riemer, Thorsten Scheibel, Tobias Pieper] XXL-Vision Medientechnik GmbH, Höchstenbach [Patrick Olivier, Stéphane Hazebrouck] **Media Control** von Aichberger & Roenneke Gesellschaft für Audiovision mbH, Cologne [Dominik Roenneke, Frank Langmann, Daniel Strücker] **Multimedia Programming** Medialab AG, Munich [Andreas Niessner, Patrick Zenker] Ingenieurbüro Andreas Niessner Multimedia Design & Consulting, Munich [Andreas Niessner] **Child Care Concept and Program Design for Audi Kids Club** kids & friends, Düsseldorf [Ruth Lintemeier, Sophie Scholz, Anne Preckel] **Photography for Visitors' activities** Michael Haase, Berlin; Ralf Kaiser, Berlin **Assembly and Exhibition Stand Photography** Hans-Georg Esch, Hennef-Stadt Blankenberg [Hans-Georg Esch, Tibor Magaslaki] Andreas Keller Fotografie, Kirchentellinsfurt [Andreas Keller, Deborah Bausch] **Reporting Photography** Sabine Klein, Munich; Astrid Prangel, Munich; Marek Vogel, Munich; Vera Nowottny, Munich

The editors thank everyone who supported the realization of this book and made it possible.

Auftrag / **Auftraggeber, Bauherr: AUDI AG, Ingolstadt** Projekt: Messestände [IAA Internationale Automobil-Ausstellung Frankfurt 1999, TMS Tokyo Motor Show 1999, NAIAS North American International Auto Show Detroit 2000, Salon International de l'Automobile de Genève 2000, Mondial de l'Automobile Paris 2000, NAIAS North American International Auto Show Detroit 2001, Salon International de l'Automobile de Genève 2001]

Konzept / **Architektur: Ingenhoven Overdiek und Partner, Düsseldorf** Wettbewerb [Christoph Ingenhoven, Hinrich Schumacher, Ralf Dorsch-Rüter, Maximo Victoria, Sylvia Domke] Projektleitung [Christoph Ingenhoven, Jürgen Overdiek, Michael Reiß] Entwurfs-, Genehmigungs- und Ausführungsplanung [Herwig Rott, Andreas Blum, Karan Djalaei, Holger Gravius, Liyang Guo, Manfred Junghans, Florian Nedden, Ingrid Sölken, Maximo Victoria, Christina Zippel] **Kommunikation: KMS Team, München** Projektleitung [Michael Keller, Christoph Rohrer, Thorsten Buch, Sabine Thernes] Projektmanagement [Sven Sonnendorfer, Angelika Mosner, Ralph Ilsanker] Gestaltung [Sabine Klein, Simone Moll, Kolja Moormann, Uschi Pfingstgraf, Tina Schmerber, Stefanie Schröder, Carolin Welß, Nerina Wilter] Text [Wolf Bruns, Dominik Neubauer] Produktion [Christina Baur, Karin Fugmann, Matthias Karpf, Angela Keesman, Bernd Müller, Christian Ring, Monika Weiglein]

Ausführung / **Generalplanung: Ingenhoven Overdiek Planungsgesellschaft GmbH & Co KG, Düsseldorf** Kosten-, Terminplanung, Ausschreibung, Vergabe [Udo Rex, Andrea Thoma, Andreas Kramer] Bauleitung, künstlerische Objektüberwachung [Udo Rex, Michael Reiß, Herwig Rott, Andrea Thoma] in Zusammenarbeit mit Severich & Partner GmbH & Co. KG, Roetgen [Karl-Heinz Severich, Rainer Glenk] **Tragwerksplanung** Werner Sobek Ingenieure GmbH, Stuttgart [Werner Sobek, Alfred Rein, Theodor Angelopoulos, Jörg Kuhn, Sandra Neaga, Ute Schenk, Klaus Straub, Arnold Walz, Ingo Weiss] **Planung Gebäudelicht** Werning Tropp Schmidt, Feldafing [Clemens Tropp, Ulrich Werning, Markus Tuppen] **Planung Ausstellungs- und Effektlicht** FOUR TO ONE: scale design GmbH, Köln [Michael Schmidt, Burkhard Jüterbock, Stephan Löper, Peter Rauscher, Elisabeth Jarych, Doreen Schlenner] **Lichttechnik** Showtec, Köln [Thomas Ickenroth, Sabine Huckenbeck, Heribert Dohm, Thomas Backhausen, Markus Boßdorf, Lars Wulff, Oliver Klaus, Ralf Berek, Frank Kähne, Volker Hardtke] Procon Multimedia AG, Glinde [Manfred Janßen, Carsten Will] **Bau- und Raumakustik** DS-Plan GmbH, Stuttgart **Personenstromanalyse** Durth Roos Consulting GmbH, Darmstadt [Thomas Weissenberger] **Brandschutz** BPK Brandschutzplanung Klingsch, Düsseldorf [Wolfram Klingsch, Gürsel Dincer] **Architekturmodelle** Amalgam Modelmakers and Designers, Bristol, UK [Anthony Pallanca, Leo Saunders] Atelier Axel Oehlschlägel, Düsseldorf [Axel Oehlschlägel] Dörre Mobau GmbH, Düsseldorf [Reinhard Dörre] Lütke Modellbau, Olching [Manfred Lütke, Renate Kässbohrer] **Illustrationen** Peter Wels, Hamburg **Modellfotografie** Studio Holger Knauf, Düsseldorf **Messebau** Ambrosius Messebau, Frankfurt am Main [Joachim Hemberger, Jürgen Franz, Harald Heidrich, Denise Mindnich, Heinz Schlosser, Sven Berthold] George P. Johnson Company, Michigan, USA [Lynn Brockmann, Michael Cherubin, Chantelle Couchie, Anthony Motto, Colleen Zalmezak] A&A Expo International BV, Wijk bij Duurstede, NL [Anton Heidemann] **Stahlbau ›Loop‹** MBM Konstruktion GmbH, Möckmühl [Peter Müller, Georg Wieland, Jürgen Bauer, Michael Fritz] Seele, Gersthofen [Gerhard Seele, Emil Rohrer] **Stahlbau Stand** Klostermair Messebau Metalltechnik Logistik, Untermaxfeld [Klaus Klostermair, Klaus Kramer, Georg Birkmeier, Peter Schwarz] SYSCON GmbH, Hockenheim [Timo Burgmeier] **Stahlbau ›Loop‹ und Stand** E&C Engineering & Construction BV, Utrecht, NL [Wim Neven, Bram de Jonge] **Werkstattplanung ›Loop‹** Alfa Plan GmbH Techniker & Ingenieure, Efringen-Kirchen [Armin Kainz, Waldemar Oswald, Klaus Volker Kniffka] **Glasverarbeitung ›Loop‹** Andreas Oswald GmbH Metallbau/Konstruktiver Glasbau, München [Bernhard Homeier, Ernst Homeier] **Produktentwicklung Teppichboden** Carpet Concept Objekt-Teppichboden GmbH, Bielefeld [Thomas Trenkamp] **Graphische Realisierung** Schüttenberg GmbH, Düsseldorf [Felix Schüttenberg, Ernst-Dieter Schüttenberg, Ralf Nieß, Jürgen Tröger, Markus Scholz, Frank Honeiker, Reza Riahi, Renate Kraatz] Reger Studios, München [Peter Knödler, Thomas Maurer] **Technische Exponate** Hüttinger Exhibition Engineering, Schwaig bei Nürnberg [Kurt Hüttinger, Armin Beck] **Showcars und technische Exponate** Uedelhoven Studios, Gaimersheim **Bekleidungskollektion Standpersonal** Mey & Edlich GmbH & Co. KG, München [Henk Fleischmann, Birgit Henniger] **Bewegungssysteme** BUMAT Bewegungssysteme GmbH, Hockenheim **Fundus Standbau** Klostermair Messebau, Untermaxfeld [Klaus Klostermair, Klaus Kramer, Georg Birkmeier, Peter Appel, Peter Schwarz] **Fundus Lichttechnik** Eschelbach Lichttechnik, Murnau am Staffelsee [Christian Eschelbach] **Fundus Interior** Herkommer + Gutbrod, Ingolstadt [Christian Leitmeier] **Bemusterung** Tischlerei Jagsch GmbH & Co. KG, Düsseldorf [Dieter Jagsch] Fries Innenausbau, Düsseldorf [Rainer Fries, Angelika Fries] **Film** velvet Mediendesign GmbH, München [Anne Böck, Arndt Buss-von Kuk, Luis Castrillo, Georgia Caramichu, Simone Haberland, Christian Künstler, Manfred Laumer, Claudius Schulz, Conny Unger, Matthias Zentner] **Musik** TTM Production, Freising [Andreas List, Jürgen Lang, Jochen Seibert] **Planung audiovisuelle Medientechnik** Michael Nicht + Partner, Schlichting [Michael Nicht, Michael Saddey, Peter Schneekloth] **Audiovisuelle Medientechnik** A.D.A.M. Showtechnik GmbH, Willroth [Jürgen Starrmann, Wulf Issinger] Amptown Verleih GmbH & Co. KG, Hamburg [Christian Tesche, Ulf Sikora, Matthias Müllenbach] Gahrens + Battermann, Bergisch Gladbach [Bernd Nössler, Stefan Müller] Lang Audiovision AG, Lindlar; mediaMotion AG, Köln [Ralf Stupp, Thomas Ahr] Neumann & Müller GmbH, München [Martin Schiller, Patrick Eckerlin] MEDIA!AG, München; PASS GmbH, Steinheim-Höpfingheim [Stefan Tulipan] Beam GmbH Communication-Systems, Soest [Hans-Georg Riemer, Thorsten Scheibel, Tobias Pieper] XXL-Vision Medientechnik GmbH, Höchstenbach [Patrick Olivier, Stéphane Hazebrouck] **Mediensteuerung** von Aichberger & Roenneke Gesellschaft für Audiovision mbH, Köln [Dominik Roenneke, Frank Langmann, Daniel Strücker] **Multimedia-Programmierung** Medialab AG, München [Andreas Niessner, Patrick Zenker] Ingenieurbüro Andreas Niessner Multimedia Design & Consulting, München [Andreas Niessner] **Konzeption und Programmgestaltung Audi Kids Club** kids & friends, Düsseldorf [Ruth Lintemeier, Sophie Scholz, Anne Preckel] **Fotografie Besucheraktion** Michael Haase, Berlin; Ralf Kaiser, Berlin **Aufbau-, Standfotografie** Hans-Georg Esch, Hennef-Stadt Blankenberg [Hans-Georg Esch, Tibor Magaslaki] Andreas Keller Fotografie, Kirchentellinsfurt [Andreas Keller, Deborah Bausch] **Reportagefotografie** Sabine Klein, München; Astrid Prangel, München; Marek Vogel, München; Vera Nowottny, München

Die Herausgeber bedanken sich bei allen, die die Realisierung dieses Buches unterstützt und ermöglicht haben.

Christoph Ingenhoven Engineer and Architect BDA **1960** Born in Düsseldorf **1978–84** Degree in Architecture, RWTH Aachen, Kunst-akademie Düsseldorf **1985** Ingenhoven Architekten Ingenieure, Düsseldorf **Since 1992** Ingenhoven Overdiek und Partner, Düsseldorf **Ingenhoven Overdiek und Partner** Since the establishment of an architectural association in 1992, the firm has been managed by Christoph Ingenhoven and Jürgen Overdiek. Together with project partners Barbara Bruder, Klaus Frankenheim, Rudolf Jonas, Klaus J. Osterburg, Michael Reiß and Hinrich Schumacher, they head a team of 85 architects as well as specialists in interior design, architectural drafting and model making. With additional staff in the areas of construction management, accounting and administration, the firm today has around 150 employees. **Areas of Concentration** Office and administrative buildings, headquarters of international companies and insurance firms, high-rise projects in Germany and abroad, department stores and infrastructure projects [airports, train stations] as well as city planning and landscape planning, product development, product design and general planning **Clients** [selection] AUDI AG, Ingolstadt; Hubert Burda Media, Munich; Canary Wharf Group PLC, London; Commerzbank AG, Frankfurt am Main; Deutsche Bahn AG, Stuttgart; Deutsche Lufthansa AG, Frankfurt am Main; Deutsche Post AG, Bonn; Dürr GmbH, Stuttgart; ECE, Hamburg; GIRA, Radevormwald; Hines, Berlin; HypoVereinsbank, Munich; Rheinland Holding, Neuss; Karstadt AG, Essen; RWE AG, Essen; Shanghai Wan Xiang International Plaza Co. Ltd., Shanghai; Stadtsparkasse Düsseldorf; Stadtwerke Düsseldorf AG; Tishman Speyer Properties, Berlin

Michael Keller Designer **1963** Born in Glendale, California, USA **1985–88** Degree in Communications Design, Munich **1988–90** Degree in Fine Arts, Parsons School of Design, New York and stipend at the Cooper Union for the Advancement of Science and Art, New York **Since 1990** Associate at KMS Team GmbH, Munich **KMS Team** was founded in 1984. The partners, Michael Keller, Knut Maierhofer and Christoph Rohrer, head a team of 60 employees, among them 30 designers. **Areas of Concentration** Brand development and corporate design, corporate and financial communications as well as trade fairs and exhibitions **Clients** [selection] ARAG Lebensversicherungs-AG, Munich; AUDI AG, Ingolstadt; Automobili Lamborghini S.p.A., Sant'Agata Bolognese; Buderus AG, Wetzlar; compær AG, Munich; Deutscher Skilehrerverband, Munich; EVOTEC BioSystems AG, Hamburg; S. Fischer Verlag, Frankfurt; KirchPayTV GmbH & Co KGaA, KirchMedia GmbH & Co KGaA, Munich; KPMG, Berlin; Mercer Management Consulting, Munich; Museum Charlotte Zander Schloss Bönnigheim; Museum Villa Stuck, Munich; Philip Morris Kunstförderung, Munich; Premiere World, Munich; ProSiebenSat.1 Media AG, Munich; Saturn Electro Handels-GmbH, Ingolstadt; SevenOne Media GmbH, Munich; VIAG Interkom GmbH & Co., Munich

Christoph Ingenhoven Dipl.-Ing. Architekt BDA **1960** geboren in Düsseldorf **1978–84** Studium der Architektur RWTH Aachen, Kunstakademie Düsseldorf **1985** Ingenhoven Architekten Ingenieure, Düsseldorf **Seit 1992** Ingenhoven Overdiek und Partner, Düsseldorf **Ingenhoven Overdiek und Partner** Das Büro wird seit der Gründung einer Architektengemeinschaft [1992] von Christoph Ingenhoven und Jürgen Overdiek geführt. Zusammen mit den Projektpartnern Barbara Bruder, Klaus Frankenheim, Rudolf Jonas, Klaus J. Osterburg, Michael Reiß und Hinrich Schumacher leiten sie ein Team von 85 Architekten, sowie Interior Designern, Bauzeichnern und Modellbauern. Mit weiteren Mitarbeitern in den Bereichen Baumanagement, Rechnungswesen und Sekretariaten arbeiten heute insgesamt ca. 150 Mitarbeiter im Büro. **Schwerpunkte der Projekte** Büro- und Verwaltungsbauten, Hauptverwaltungen für Konzerne und Versicherungen, Hochhausprojekte im In- und Ausland, Warenhausprojekte und Infrastrukturprojekte [Flughäfen, Bahnhöfe] sowie städtebauliche Planungen und Landschaftsplanung, Produktentwicklung, Produktdesign und Generalplanung **Bauherren und Auftraggeber** [Auswahl] AUDI AG, Ingolstadt; Hubert Burda Media, München; Canary Wharf Group PLC, London; Commerzbank AG, Frankfurt am Main; Deutsche Bahn AG, Stuttgart; Deutsche Lufthansa AG, Frankfurt am Main; Deutsche Post AG, Bonn; Dürr GmbH, Stuttgart; ECE, Hamburg; GIRA, Radevormwald; Hines, Berlin; HypoVereinsbank, München; Rheinland Holding, Neuss; Karstadt AG, Essen; RWE AG, Essen; Shanghai Wan Xiang International Plaza Co. Ltd., Shanghai; Stadtsparkasse Düsseldorf; Stadtwerke Düsseldorf AG; Tishman Speyer Properties, Berlin

Michael Keller Designer **1963** geboren in Glendale, Kalifornien, USA **1985–88** Studium Kommunikationsdesign in München **1988–90** Kunststudium an der Parsons School of Design, New York, und Stipendium an der Cooper Union for the Advancement of Science and Art, New York **Seit 1990** Geschäftsführer KMS Team GmbH, München **KMS Team** wurde 1984 gegründet. Die Gesellschafter Michael Keller, Knut Maierhofer und Christoph Rohrer leiten ein Team von 60 Mitarbeitern, davon 30 Designer. **Schwerpunkte der Arbeit** Markenentwicklung und Corporate Design, Unternehmens- und Finanzkommunikation sowie Messen und Ausstellungen **Auftraggeber** [Auswahl] ARAG Lebensversicherungs-AG, München; AUDI AG, Ingolstadt; Automobili Lamborghini S.p.A., Sant'Agata Bolognese; Buderus AG, Wetzlar; compær AG, München; Deutscher Skilehrerverband, München; EVOTEC BioSystems AG, Hamburg; S. Fischer Verlag, Frankfurt am Main; KirchPayTV GmbH & Co KGaA, KirchMedia GmbH & Co KGaA, München; KPMG, Berlin; Mercer Management Consulting, München; Museum Charlotte Zander Schloss Bönnigheim; Museum Villa Stuck, München; Philip Morris Kunstförderung, München; Premiere World, München; ProSiebenSat.1 Media AG, München; Saturn Electro Handels-GmbH, Ingolstadt; SevenOne Media GmbH, München; VIAG Interkom GmbH & Co., München

Illustrations / **von Aichberger & Roenneke** Cologne: 054 **Otl Aicher** »gehen in der wüste«, S. Fischer Verlag, Frankfurt am Main 1982 [Cover]: 012 r. **Sophia and Stefan Behling** »Sol Power. Die Evolution der solaren Architektur«, Prestel-Verlag, Munich – New York 1996 [p. 200]: 008 r., [p. 234]: 011 r. **Hans-Georg Esch** Hennef-Stadt Blankenberg: 027 r., 032, 035 l., 038, 062 l., 070–073, 077, 078 r., 082, 090 l., 105 r. **Felice Frankel and George M. Whitesides** »On the Surface of Things. Images of the extraordinary in science«, Chronicle Books, San Francisco 1997 [p. 48]: 010 l., [p. 86]: 012 l. **»Future Systems. For inspiration only«**, Academy Group LTD, London 1996 [p. 122]: 007, [p. 30]: 013 **Glanzmann, Bildagentur zefa** Düsseldorf: 008 l. **Michael Haase/Ralf Kaiser** Berlin: 103 r., 104 **Ingenhoven Overdiek und Partner** Düsseldorf: 014–023, 026, 029, 030, 050, 052, 061, 064, 074, 080 r., 081 l., 097 **Andreas Keller** Kirchentellinsfurt: 075, 083, 087 **Sabine Klein** Munich: 004–006, 035 r., 041, 059, 067, 069, 095 l., 107 **KMS Team** Munich: Cover, 038, 046 r.–049, 053, 078 l., 084, 085 l., 088, 089, 091, 092, 105 l. **Holger Knauf** Düsseldorf: 024, 033, 042 r., 043 **Andreas List** Freising: 055–058 »Bäume und Gräser. Photographien von **Shinzo Maeda**«, Benedikt Taschen-Verlag, Cologne 1983 [p. 61]: 010 r. **Florian Monheim** Meerbusch: 009 **Vera Nowottny** Munich: 034, 036, 040, 041, 044 l., 054, 067, 076, 079, 080 l., 081, 086 r., 093, 100 l., 103 l., 107, 108 **Astrid Prangel** Munich: 098, 100 r.–102, 104 **Werner Sobek Ingenieure** Stuttgart: 025, 027 l., 028, 031, 060 l. **Stockmarket Bildagentur** Düsseldorf: 011 l. **velvet Mediendesign** Munich: 051, 106 r. **Visitec** Grevesmühlen: 045 **Marek Vogel** Munich: 037–039, 044 r., 046 l., 060 r., 062 r., 063, 065–068, 085 r., 086 l., 090 r., 094, 095 r., 096, 099, 106 l., 107 **Robert Wilson** New York: 001–003

We have made every effort fully and correctly to list all names, places, sources as well as other data and references to the best of our knowledge and with a safe conscience. In case information is nevertheless missing, we ask that the editors be contacted directly.